The Nature Book

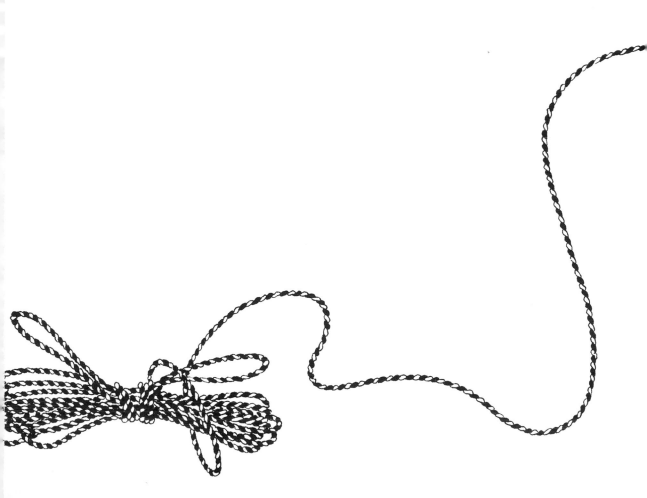

The Nature Book

**Discovering, Exploring
Observing, Experimenting
With Plants and Animals
at Home and Outdoors**

By Midas Dekkers
Illustrated by Angela de Vrede

Macmillan/McGraw-Hill School Publishing Company
New York Chicago Columbus

Macmillan Publishing Company
866 Third Avenue, New York, NY 10022
First published in Great Britain
by Exley Publications
First American edition 1988
For information regarding permission, write to
Macmillan Publishing Company
866 Third Avenue, New York, NY 10022.
This edition is reprinted by arrangement with
Macmillan Publishing Company.

Macmillan/McGraw-Hill School Division
10 Union Square East
New York, New York 10003

Printed and bound in Mexico.
ISBN 0-02-274958-6
   3 4 5 6 7 8 9 REY 99 98 97 96

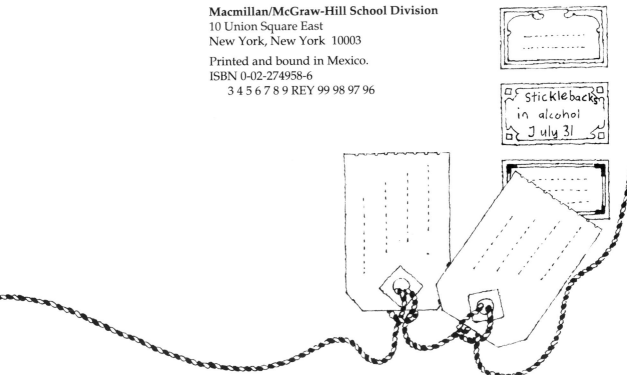

CONTENTS

At the end of the book you'll find an alphabetical index, to help you look up things in this book.

NATURE DAY BY DAY

We cry a bit all the time without really realizing it; the "tears" keep our eyes clean by washing away the dirt. During the night, the dirt washed away by the tears gathers in the corner of your eye and forms the white stuff that you rub away in the mornings when you wake up. Our tear glands slow down when we're asleep. So do our lungs, our stomachs, and our heartbeats. When we are asleep and our bodies are hardly having to do anything, our temperature and blood pressure fall too.

We sleep away a third of our lives. Shame. There may be times when you don't even feel sleepy but have to go to bed anyway because it's bedtime, because the clock says so, because everything – waking up, eating breakfast, going to school, watching television, going to bed – is ruled by the clock.

Imagine there were no clocks and nobody knew what the time was. Then you'd go to bed when you felt like it, but would you sleep less? Research has been done on this. For several weeks people were put in a room without windows, without a clock or watch, without a radio and without any light coming in from outside. The human guinea pigs didn't know what time they went to bed and got up, but the researcher did. What happened was that they lived just as they would have done at home: sleeping for eight hours, up for sixteen hours, sleeping for eight hours, up for another sixteen, and so on. They ate and went to the toilet at the same times. Had they

smuggled in a clock? In a way. We're all born with a sort of built-in clock which tells us when we're hungry or sleepy. Under normal circumstances, this biological clock tallies with mechanical clocks. It can be upset though if you do something like fly east or west to another continent. When you arrive at the airport, the clock might tell you it's late afternoon while the clock inside you tells you that it's definitely time for bed. You'll probably feel a bit under the weather for a few days until you are your old self again. (This is what is known as jet lag.) All plants and animals have built-in biological clocks and they go to sleep at a fixed time each day. Flowers fold up their petals, cabbage grows more slowly, animals retire to their nests and dens. They don't all sleep at the same time; some retire at night, others in the daytime. Bats, burglars and moths are night-owls, up and about while chickens, law-abiding citizens and butterflies sleep. One group works by the light of the stars, the other in sunlight. Sun and stars move across the sky from hour to hour, from day to day, and from east to west. It takes a year for them to return to more or less the same position as before. Our division of time into years is centuries-old, based on the movements of the sun and the stars. Calendars are just as important to our lives as clocks: lazy days in the summer, the dreaded exams, Christmas on December 25. It's comforting to know that plants and animals also follow a kind of calendar; they die too. When the summer dies, so do most insects. Many plants wither down into the soil and trees shed their leaves. Deep in the ground, seeds and tiny eggs wait for warmer days. Migratory birds leave for warmer or cooler climes. How do they know that the time has come for all this? It isn't because they're hungry. On the contrary, they need full stomachs by the time they leave in order to survive the long journey. Do birds keep to a secret yearly plan? Yes, of sorts. All over the colder areas of the world, they notice the days shortening and the nights drawing in as winter approaches, and it makes them restless. Eventually, when they can bear it no longer, they leave, flying to escape the cold of winter. (Human beings often do the unnatural thing by going to the hottest beaches for their summer break at a time when the weather at home is at its warmest. Then when winter comes, they huddle close to the fire or radiator, complaining about the heating bills!) Once spring comes to the colder areas of the world, the worst is behind, and life begins again. Birds return, seeds germinate and we humans do our spring-cleaning. Spring brings light and warmth. Light gives the plants new energy. Warmth speeds up life; a rise in temperature of ten degrees makes the processes inside a plant or animal twice as quick.

Because seasons change, spring blossoming into summer flowers, the leaves falling until the cold arrives, nature is different every day, and things only return to about the same state after a year. It's never absolutely the same because the weather varies a little each year, and plants and animals never behave exactly as they did the previous year. It's interesting to compare these variations. When did the oak buds burst last year? When did the blackbirds' eggs hatch? Is the sunflower taller than last year? You'll need to consult nature's last year's calendar to find out. This isn't as impossible as it sounds, not if you've been keeping the calendar yourself, as a logbook. Every day write down what you see in the natural world around you.

Keeping a logbook

You learn by using both eyes and hands. Note down everything you see so that you remember it. Otherwise you'll forget and that would be a pity. If you don't remember, it will be because you didn't record all the details you first noticed.

Keep a note of everything you see. Any hardbound notebook will do – or a ring-binder with a hard cover. Start each day on a new page. At the top, write down the date and then note, for example:
– what the weather's like
– where you've been
– how your experiments are coming along
– the places where you've found things (they're called stations)
– anything relevant that you've seen in a book

Use the book to draw in too, as often as you can. Drawing makes you look at things more closely. Do you know exactly what shape a honeysuckle flower is, or its leaves? Or how many legs a wood-louse has? You would if you'd drawn them. You don't have to be good at drawing, just good at noticing. You don't have to draw everything yourself either. You can always stick in pictures cut out from magazines, as well as birds' feathers, leaves, and other flat objects. Your logbook will grow each day, and the longer you keep it, the more valuable it becomes, till one day it'll be even more priceless than a library full of books, because it'll be all your own work, your own history.

aquarium : 24 baby fish left, 14 pale, pale orange

T.V. film about cuttle fish laying eggs

brown

white band

black

whiskers

white tummy

Spotted a big new cat
name: "whiskers"
walks low on her paws (scared?)

Tuesday July 3

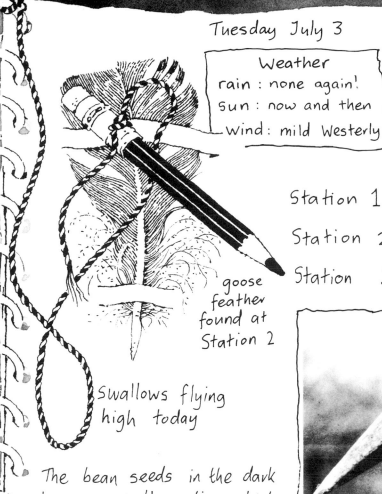

Weather
rain : none again!
sun : now and then
wind: mild Westerly

Walked in park, saw:
pigeon
blue jay
magpie
robin
heard a woodpecker

Station 1 : park behind ice-cream
stand
Station 2 : park at pond
Station 3 : school playground
under oak tree

goose feather found at Station 2

Swallows flying high today

The bean seeds in the dark have grown three times higher than the seeds in the light. The onion has a flower bud.

Masie the marabou stork

Chicken pulling worm out of the ground.

Cat - 7:15am let her in

2 - 4:30 pm slept (in Sun)

fought Redbeard and lost again!

6pm fed her. Plate emptied in 2½ mins

Caught 12 fleas with comb.

Your own weather station

Plants and animals don't have clothes and fires and umbrellas. Their lives are run by the weather, much more than ours are. Butterflies need warmth; on a cold day they can't fly upwards. Plants need sun; snails are happiest in a shower. If you want to find out what's going on in nature, you'll first need to know what the weather's like. There's the weather forecast on the radio, of course, but that always covers a whole region, not just the area around your house. Only your own weather station will be reliable enough. From now on, keep a weather record in your logbook every day.

Temperature, wind, precipitation (rain, snow, hail) and atmospheric pressure together make up the weather. Wind and precipitation can be measured with home-made apparatus, but you'll need to buy a thermometer and barometer for temperature and pressure. Hang the thermometer out of the sun and at shoulder-height off the ground.

You can see from your barometer whether the pressure is rising (means fine weather) or falling (bad weather). Your eyes are really the best meters. Look up at the sky. High rippling cirrus clouds mean fine weather; cumulus clouds piled up in a heap mean poor weather. Look at the sky in the evening and think of the old proverb: "Red sky at night, shepherd's delight; red sky in the morning, shepherd's warning."

Make a windsock from a scrap of thin material 15 by 20 inches (40 x 50 cms.). Cut out a shape like the one in the picture. Fold, and sew the two long sides together. Make a circle of some firm wire, and sew it into the wider end, having first slotted two rings on to it; these should be opposite each other. Put a steel pin – a metal knitting needle would do – through the two rings and then mount this axle on a pole in which you have already bored a hole. Put a wooden bead between the pole and the lower ring, so that the sock is able to move around freely in the wind. Mark on the pole where North, South, East and West are. When the wind fills the sock, look at this gauge to see which way the sock is pointing, i.e. the direction of the wind.

10

Swallows flying high means good weather. This is because swallows live on insects and when warm air rises it carries the insects up with it. The swallows follow. In poor weather, insects and swallows fly closer to the ground. Worms, snails and slugs will be crawling there because of the damp. If the cows are running restlessly around the field, tails raised, nostrils flared, there's going to be a thunderstorm; the cows are trying to escape the vicious bites from the horse-flies and hornets which are particularly active before a storm.

Compare the temperature reading on your thermometer when it's just off the ground. and when it's at the height of your shoulder. There's quite a difference!

All you need to measure precipitation is a jar and a filter. Find a filter whose circumference at the top is as wide as the bottom of the jar, and put it into the neck of the jar. Paint a measuring scale down the side of the jar and your rain gauge is ready.

Watch the plants. If the bindweed flowers stay open, the weather will stay warm. In dry weather the scales of pine-cones stick out, and they close up when it is damp. Seaweed's firm when the weather's dry, floppy when it's wet.

Helping your eyes and hands

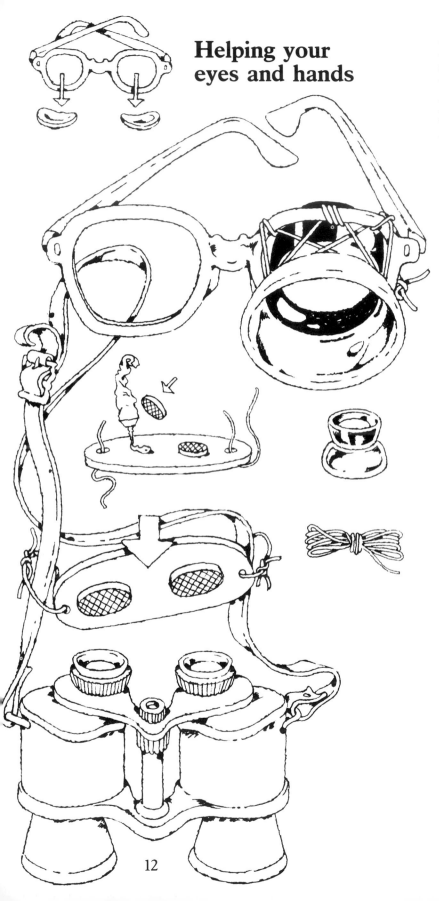

Nature researchers need to do a lot of looking and picking things up. Sometimes eyes and hands are not enough and you need help.

Without a magnifying glass, you won't be able to see insect feet properly, or flower stamens or the scales on butterfly wings. A magnifying glass should magnify about ten times. You can buy a plastic eye glass quite cheaply at a photographic shop. Since you'll need to hold it close to your eye, why not make a pair of magnifying spectacles? Take the lenses out of an old pair of glasses and fix a magnifying eye glass to one side with a piece of string or plastic glue.

Although birds, squirrels and deer are large enough to be seen with the naked eye if you're close enough, sometimes this isn't possible, and you'll need binoculars. The most useful binoculars are 7 x 50; the figures will be marked on them. The first figure refers to the magnification factor: seven times. Don't get stronger ones because they make the picture wobble and you'll need a stand to keep it steady. The second number is the measurement of the thickness of the lenses in front: 50 mm. When you're out on an expedition carry the binoculars around your neck and leave the case at home; it'll only get in the way. Protect the lenses at the looking end with a cover which will slide down over them automatically (see picture on left). Make this cover from cardboard and cover it with plastic or synthetic leather.

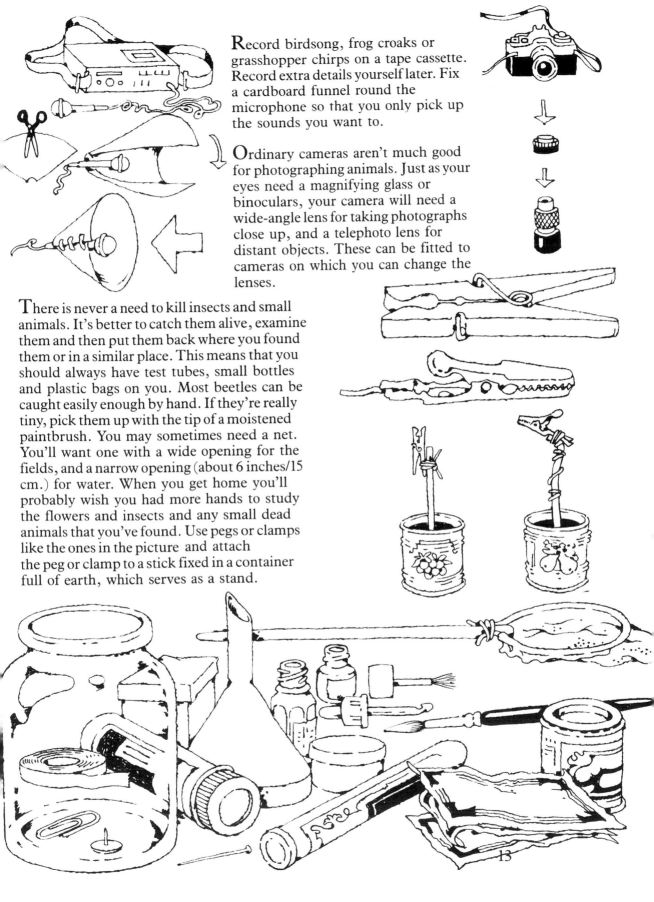

Record birdsong, frog croaks or grasshopper chirps on a tape cassette. Record extra details yourself later. Fix a cardboard funnel round the microphone so that you only pick up the sounds you want to.

Ordinary cameras aren't much good for photographing animals. Just as your eyes need a magnifying glass or binoculars, your camera will need a wide-angle lens for taking photographs close up, and a telephoto lens for distant objects. These can be fitted to cameras on which you can change the lenses.

There is never a need to kill insects and small animals. It's better to catch them alive, examine them and then put them back where you found them or in a similar place. This means that you should always have test tubes, small bottles and plastic bags on you. Most beetles can be caught easily enough by hand. If they're really tiny, pick them up with the tip of a moistened paintbrush. You may sometimes need a net. You'll want one with a wide opening for the fields, and a narrow opening (about 6 inches/15 cm.) for water. When you get home you'll probably wish you had more hands to study the flowers and insects and any small dead animals that you've found. Use pegs or clamps like the ones in the picture and attach the peg or clamp to a stick fixed in a container full of earth, which serves as a stand.

13

Star gazing

You really don't need a telescope to look at the stars; your eyes are perfectly adequate. Just look: stars galore. Learn which they are and go on to discover planets too. With a pair of binoculars you'll be able to see mountains and plains on the moon as clearly as in the pictures of an atlas.

When you first gaze up at the stars, they just look like a blur of little dots, a bit like the haze of light hanging over a strange city at night. Birds understand this haze; they use the stars to guide them when they migrate, but human beings need a map of the constellations. Some stars, like Perseus, were named centuries ago after mythological characters; others were named after animals. A constellation is a group of stars which, when seen from the Earth, seem to make a shape or picture. It's useful to know the constellations in finding one's way round the skies.

Start by letting your eyes grow accustomed to the dark. Gradually, you'll see more stars. Look to the north for a conspicuous constellation called Ursa Major (Great or Big Bear). An imaginary line through the two brightest stars points to the North Star (Polaris), which lies in Ursa Minor (Little Bear). Ursa Minor is a small faint constellation. The North Star is the only star to stay in the same place (almost exactly in the north). The other stars all seem to circle around the North Star.

In fact it isn't the stars which move, it's the Earth. The Earth turns on its axis once every twenty-four hours, and circles the sun once every 365 days. This makes it look to us as if the stars are in a certain position four minutes earlier each night, almost half an hour earlier each week. Wait until one star disappears right behind the corner of your home. Write down what the time is. Stand in exactly the same spot a week later and look for the same star. This time it'll go behind the corner half an hour earlier. Sometimes you'll see bright stars which don't circle with the others and which you can't find on any astronomical chart. That's because these "wild stars" are planets. Venus and Jupiter are the brightest; Mars is the red one. You may be able to see Jupiter's moons with your binoculars. Aim them at the central star on the "tail" of the Bear in Ursa Major, and you'll find that what you thought was one star are two. The Milky Way (a broad band of light going across the sky) breaks down into thousands of stars when seen through binoculars. Sometimes a star seems to fall from the sky. Although we call these shooting stars, they aren't really; they're meteorites which hurtle across the sky at a speed of 130,000 m.p.h. and burn themselves out in the atmosphere. The best time to see shooting stars is between August 10 and 15, when they shoot out in bundles from the Perseus constellation. Keep track in your logbook of how many you see in one hour in the evenings between those dates.

The dark patches on the moon are called seas. Here are the names of some of them:
1. Sea of Rains
2. Ocean of Storms
3. Sea of Clouds
4. Sea of Moisture
5. Sea of Serenity
6. Sea of Crises
7. Sea of Tranquility
In fact they aren't seas at all but arid plains. The first man on the moon landed in the Sea of Tranquility.

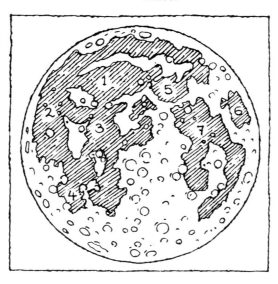

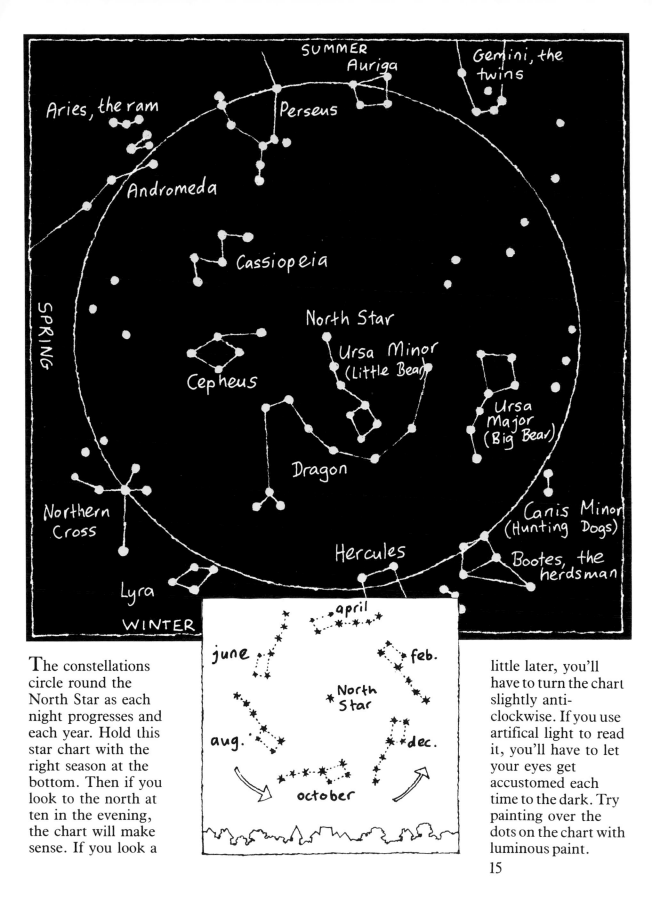

The constellations circle round the North Star as each night progresses and each year. Hold this star chart with the right season at the bottom. Then if you look to the north at ten in the evening, the chart will make sense. If you look a little later, you'll have to turn the chart slightly anti-clockwise. If you use artifical light to read it, you'll have to let your eyes get accustomed each time to the dark. Try painting over the dots on the chart with luminous paint.

15

COLLECTING

Some people collect stamps or antiques, others collect long-playing records or good marks for their school projects. Everyone collects something from nature at some time in their lives. Have you ever picked up an acorn or a shell and put it in your pocket?

Sooner or later, most acorns and shells in pockets end up being thrown out, just as they should be; there's no point in acorns or shells gathering dust in pockets! Collections are only worth anything once you do something with them. They should be sorted out, everything in its own group: tiny skulls with tiny skulls, feathers with feathers, mice with mice and birds with birds. Then your collection has something unique, something which does not exist in the natural state where plants and animals are scrambled up together, not separated out neatly. The order that you bring to the collection helps you to discover all sorts of things. If, for instance, you want to put leaves together according to type, you may suddenly notice a difference between two leaves which you had previously thought were exactly the same. Collecting makes you look more closely. In fact, the most important discoveries about plants and animals have been made by collectors. The Swede, Carl Linnaeus, was one famous collector; in the eighteenth century he kept a sort of stamp album of all the plants and animals that he knew. The more two sorts resembled one another, the closer he put them together. One interesting thing which came out of this, was that coloration is not very important. If you put red flowers beside other red flowers, you'll get a hodge-podge of roses and geraniums; or of cornflowers and forget-me-nots if the flowers are blue. It's structure that counts, not even subtle shading.

A century later, Charles Darwin made an even more important contribution than Linnaeus. He asked himself *why* some sorts seemed to go together while others did not. After years of collecting, sorting and thinking, he knew the answer: two kinds which resemble each other are part of the same family, not brothers and sisters but fifth cousins, all coming from the same set of parents millions of years ago. Since then, they've grown more and more different from each other, more apart, but you can still see that they're related. Darwin called this evolution. Lions and tigers look similar because they come from the same primeval cats. Why do you think human beings look like apes?

When you begin collecting you start to discover things. Nature will already have done some of the sorting out for you: dark feathers along the water's edge, rabbit skulls in fields, owl pellets at the foot of a tree, wood-lice under stones. When you get home, clean your finds and arrange them. Now comes the important part; the first step in getting to know them is to find out their names. It's just the same with people, except that plants and animals won't tell you their names so you'll need to ask someone who knows about such things, or to compare them with pictures in books until you finally identify them. It really is worth buying a few good field guides if you're interested in nature; they'll last you for life. Some of these guidebooks have a key as well as pictures. Use the key by choosing between two descriptions again and again, until you end up with the name of the object you're looking for. You may go wrong at the beginning, especially with plants which look like grass or a dandelion. It's easier if you start with flowers whose petals and stamens and pistils you can count. When you've put a name to a plant or animal, you'll be able to look them up and find out how they live.

Some people are so fond of collecting animals that they kill them! This really is unnecessary. There are plenty of dead animals that you can find, like flies on the window sill, mice killed by a cat, tiny birds fallen from the nest, dead fish from your pond. Most of the things you find on the beach are dead as a dodo too. If your family eats fish or animals you can use these for study too. You can pick flowers – but only if there are plenty of them. Don't pick rare kinds. The more common flowers are perfectly adequate for your purposes. If you want to go in for rare objects, then you should be collecting stamps or antiques! In fact, some plants and animals – like orchids, and a lot of birds – are so rare that they're protected. People are forbidden to touch them. You can still collect them but you'll have to limit yourself to their names. At the back of your logbook make a list of all the birds you've seen; the list will get longer each time you see a new type. In

this way you'll be collecting names instead of tiny corpses. Have a competition with a friend to see who can collect the most. Even this isn't the most important thing. It isn't collecting objects and names which matters, but collecting facts. Each time you find something new, or something happens which you've never seen before, you're adding something to the most important and largest collection: your knowledge of nature.

An expedition jacket

Long ago there used to be a strip cartoon character who went searching for butterflies and flowers in a top hat and tails. When he found something he wanted to keep, he pinned it to his hat!

We're going to be more sensible and make an expedition jacket, full of pockets and gadgets to make it as useful as possible.

Anything you might need on your expedition is going to be in or attached to your jacket, in pockets, fitted through loops, or attached to hooks. This will mean that your hands are always kept free.

If you're going to make the jacket make it from denim or some other tough cotton. Green or brown are the least conspicuous out-of-doors but jeans blue is all right: most animals can't see the difference anyway. You can always adapt a jacket you've got already; all you'll need to do is sew on pockets and loops. Old jackets often have all sorts of pockets and things in them anyway.

How your jacket will look depends on how tall you are and what you want to take with you. It's probably best to start with a simple jacket and add pockets and loops as they're needed. What matters is to give all your things a place of their own so that you know exactly where they are when you need them.

These are the sort of things you might want on your jacket:

– An *inside pocket* for your *logbook.* It's the most important thing you'll be carrying, and you'll need to keep it dry.

– *Labels.* Label everything, stating where and when you found it. When you find a lot of things in one spot, give the place a number and label everything from there with that number. When you get home, you'll be able to look up the number in your logbook to see where the "station" (which is what biologists call such a place) was. For example: station 7: grandma's farm, behind the hedge.

– A *pencil.* More useful than a pen because ink runs in the rain. Labels written in pencil can be read even in water or alcohol. Take a pencil-sharpener too!

– *Plenty of jars, test tubes and boxes* to put your finds in, whether dead or alive. You can examine live insects in the test tubes, and use jars as traps (see p.74). Stick some *pins* in your jacket too, they're useful for prodding and poking.

– *Alcohol* or *formaldehyde* is useful for preserving worms and water creatures (see p.20). So make sure that you fill some test tubes before setting off. (Don't drink it! And remember it's inflammable!)

– *A magnifying glass or magnifying glasses* (see p.12). You could hang the eye-glass on a string round your neck.

– *A pocket flashlight* comes in handy for looking at a wood-louse and other nocturnal creatures (see p.75). Many of these are attracted by the light; others are repelled by it.

– *Plastic bags* are not only for keeping things in. They'll also keep your stuff dry when it's raining.

– *A cleat lock* (like the lock on a dog's leash) attached to the shoulder of the jacket will be useful for hanging things from, *a net* or *coil of rope,* for example.

– Roll up *a piece of white cloth* and take it, if you've room. When you spread it out you'll be amazed at the number of insects that'll head straight for it and land on it.

– Other things which are useful are: a *spoon,* a *strainer* (see p.75), *tweezers,* a *penknife,* a *tapemeasure, scissors* and … *Band-Aids!*

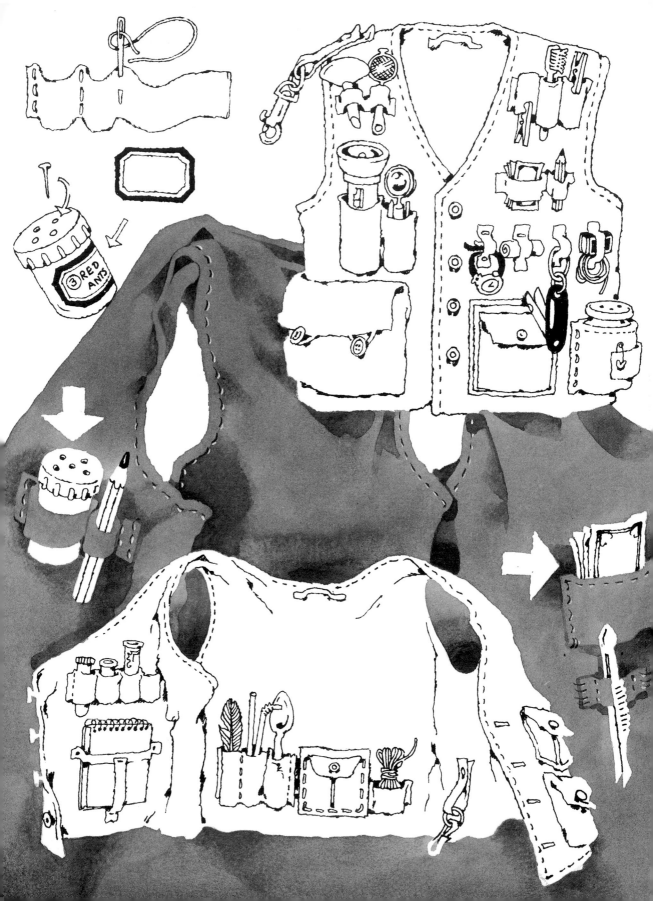

A museum of your own

You can put your finds in your own museum. That is, the ones that are worth keeping. Bacteria and fungi are constantly on the lookout for dead plants and animals, which is useful in nature but not in a museum, so your booty will need to be kept properly or your museum will become a stinking mess in no time at all.

Shells and *bones* are the easiest to keep because they are made of calcium which bacteria and fungi do not like. All you need to do is thoroughly clean the shells (see p.24) and bones (see p.28). The same applies to *sea-urchin* and *crab* shells.

If you find dead *insects*, then display them by piercing them with pins. Use stainless steel pins so that they don't rust. Bend the insects' legs and antennae into the correct position. If this is difficult because the insect has been dead for some time then try first laying it in a closed jar lined with some wet toilet paper.

Display all the insects on pins in a closed box with a floor of white soft board or firm polystyrene.

Insects from ditches, dead *fish* from your aquarium, *worms* and *spiders* need to be preserved in alcohol (70%) or formaldehyde. You can buy these at a pharmacy. Close the jars tightly because alcohol and formaldehyde quickly evaporate and they are also inflammable.

Only keep the skeletons (see p.28) and feathers (with a mothball) of *birds.* You can keep both the skeleton and the skin of *small mammals* (dead vole or a mouse brought in by the cat). Do what Davy Crockett and the trappers used to do. Slit the skin down the belly from chin to tail, and loosen it from the body with scissors, penknife and tweezers. Make a tanning solution by dissolving 100 g. table salt and 100 g. alum in a quart of boiling water. When the solution is cool, put the skin in to soak for a day and a night. Then stretch it across a wooden frame, sewing the edges to the frame with string. Scrape away as much fat and flesh as you can from the inside and give it a final brushdown.

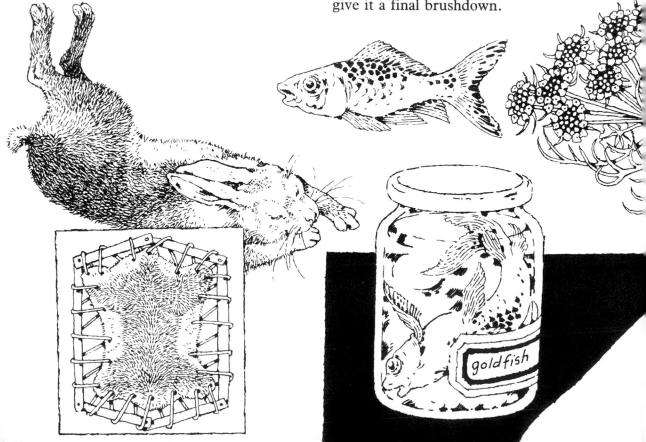

goldfish

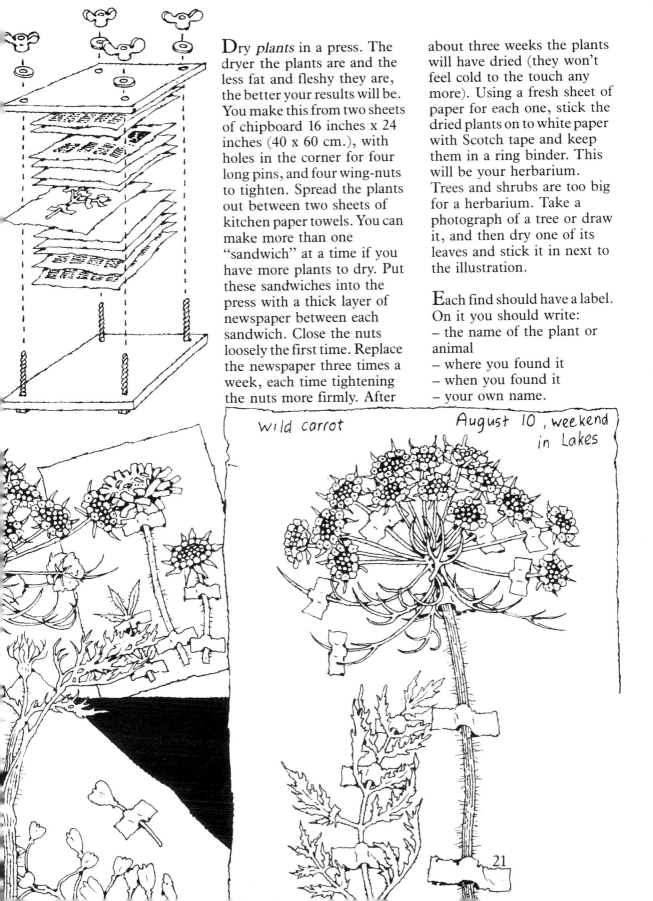

Dry *plants* in a press. The dryer the plants are and the less fat and fleshy they are, the better your results will be. You make this from two sheets of chipboard 16 inches x 24 inches (40 x 60 cm.), with holes in the corner for four long pins, and four wing-nuts to tighten. Spread the plants out between two sheets of kitchen paper towels. You can make more than one "sandwich" at a time if you have more plants to dry. Put these sandwiches into the press with a thick layer of newspaper between each sandwich. Close the nuts loosely the first time. Replace the newspaper three times a week, each time tightening the nuts more firmly. After about three weeks the plants will have dried (they won't feel cold to the touch any more). Using a fresh sheet of paper for each one, stick the dried plants on to white paper with Scotch tape and keep them in a ring binder. This will be your herbarium. Trees and shrubs are too big for a herbarium. Take a photograph of a tree or draw it, and then dry one of its leaves and stick it in next to the illustration.

Each find should have a label. On it you should write:
– the name of the plant or animal
– where you found it
– when you found it
– your own name.

wild carrot

August 10, weekend in Lakes

21

Going to the zoo

Animals in a museum have something missing: their normal actions in their natural surroundings. Zoos are museums for live animals, where you can go and watch how animals behave. Most people don't understand much of what they see, because they try to look at too many animals in one visit. It's better to concentrate on one animal at a time. Start with the monkey enclosure. There's plenty to see there.

Monkeys live in the trees where they are safe from leopards and other enemies. Baboons, however, stay firmly on the ground and live in tightly-knit groups for security. These groups have a strict hierarchy with a boss, a deputy boss and a deputy deputy boss. You'll be able to see this in action if the rocks where the monkeys, apes and baboons are kept at your local zoo cover a wide enough area.

Who's the boss over whom? Watch the monkeys and you'll soon find out.
– When two monkeys (or apes or baboons) pass one another, the one lower down the social scale gives way to the one which is higher.
– When food is thrown and happens to land between two monkeys, the senior one will take it and eat it; the other will hardly dare look.
– At feeding time, the senior ones take up the best positions; the junior ones sit behind and when they do eat, they keep casting anxious glances over their shoulders.
– Monkeys often show each other their rear ends. In humans, this would be an insult, but that isn't the case with monkeys where the one showing its bottom is acknowledging that the other is his superior.

Adult males are at the top of the hierarchy. Most adult male baboons can easily be spotted by the cape of long hair over their shoulders. Each has his own harem of wives. Which wife belongs to which male? Once the master of the harem starts walking, all his mates follow him. How many harems are in your local colony? Some female baboons have a swollen red bottom. Males don't.

Select one harem from a troop of baboons. How high does the master of the harem stand in the male hierarchy? How many females has he and how many children? Estimate the ages of the young baboons in this way:
– Baboons are black for the first four months, then they turn brown.
– The young ones hang from the mother's belly in the first weeks. Later they ride on her back, lying at first then sitting or standing too (*right*).
– Males only get their hoods when they are about three years old, and their heads turn lighter once they reach adulthood.

Monkeys groom each other even though they don't have fleas. The grooming is partly to keep the fur clean, partly out of friendliness. Who grooms whom?

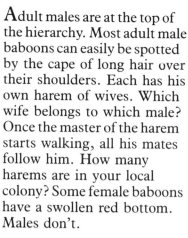

23

Beachcombing

The sea's full of surprises. Some of them will land right at your feet as you stand waiting on the beach. All you need to do is pick them up.

The best time to find shells is just after high tide, especially when there's been a storm. Whole banks of them are thrown up together. Look for them in seaweed too, and on pieces of driftwood which may have come from miles away. Many of the flat shells you find will in fact only be half of a double shell, a bi-valve. The two halves of these shells make a sort of hinged box to protect the creature inside. Examine a complete bi-valve and see how good the hinge is with its teeth and holes. A snail's shell comes in one piece. Saw carefully through it with a hacksaw to see the beautiful spiral staircase inside. Sometimes little creatures may still be inside the shells.

Wind coming off the sea throws up driftwood. Wind coming off the land is better for throwing up shells (see diagram) because the surface of the water blown away from the land streams back along the sea bed where the shells are.

When you bring the shells home, clean them under running water with an old toothbrush, soak them in a bowl of fresh water for a day and then leave them to dry. If you want to keep a bi-valve shell as a box, put a rubber band round it while it's drying. If there are parts of an animal still inside, you'll have to scrape them out. The easiest way to do this is first to put the shell into a pan of boiled water. Leave it in until the water has cooled and then start cleaning it. When you have cleaned and dried the shells, you'll find they don't look as beautiful as when they're on the beach. Rubbing with a little salad oil helps.

Now you can start building your own shell museum. Put each tiny shell into a small box and stick the boxes together to make a miniature chest of drawers. Larger shells should be displayed in a drawer with compartments. Label each shell.

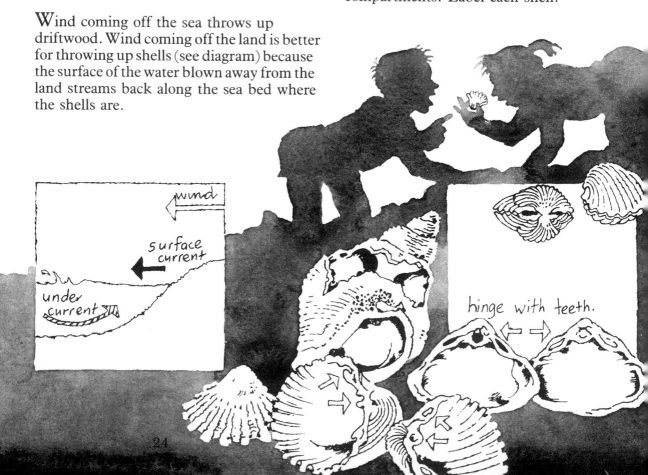

wind

surface current

under current

hinge with teeth.

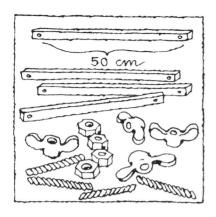
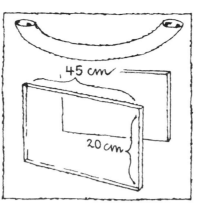
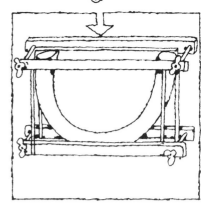

Living sea creatures are best seen in a "cuvette": two sheets of glass with a piece of transparent plastic tubing in between. Fix it together with wood and screws so that it is watertight. Pour water into the tube and then add the animals and observe them.

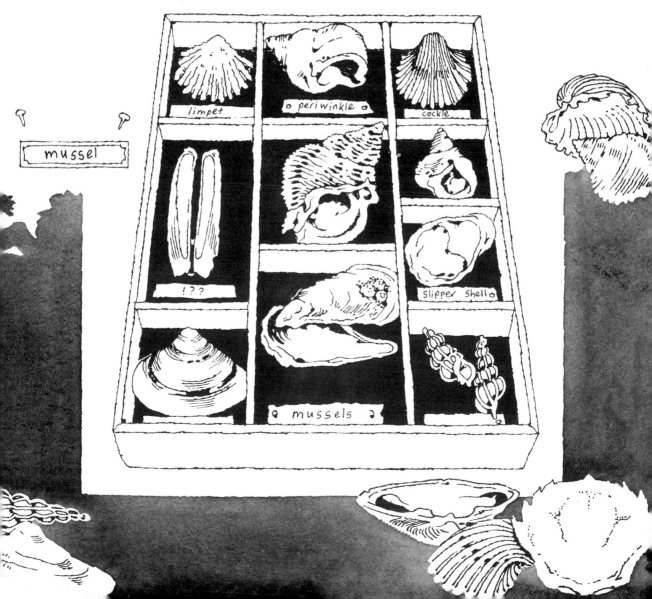

limpet

periwinkle

cockle

mussel

!??

slipper shell

mussels

FOOD IS NATURE TOO

No matter how expensive a car is, it still needs some kind of fuel to be of any use. Just like cars, open fires run on coal and wood. What about human beings? We run on boiled eggs, bread, radishes, peanut butter, apple pie, all sorts of things. People run on food. Food, like all fuels, contains energy and that energy is released when it is burned up. Just as you get heat and light by burning wood, your body gets energy by burning food. Sounds odd, doesn't it? Can you imagine a lettuce leaf burning? Well it does, once it has been processed by your intestines. After that it's burned up all round your body, and the fumes come out through your mouth. Although you don't see flames, the food does give off heat as it burns. Take your temperature: it's normally 37°C or 98.6°F, which is much warmer than your surroundings. When these surroundings are cold, your built-in stove needs to be stoked up more than it does in the warmth. That's why we often eat heavier foods, like fruit cake, in winter. The fattier and sweeter the food, the more energy it contains, and the fatter you'll become if you don't use up that energy. That's why diet books always have lists for you to look up the amount of energy contained in various foods. This energy is measured in calories. If you compare the energy in food with other sources of energy, you'll start looking at an apple or a hamburger with more respect. There's enough energy in an apple to boil a quart of water, and there's five times that amount in a cheeseburger. Ice-cream contains as much energy as a stick of dynamite! Then why aren't there more accidents at mealtime? Because energy is released only slowly from apples and ice-cream, whereas a flame put to a stick of dynamite releases it all in a fraction of a second, and makes an awful explosion.

Even so, there's less energy in food than in petroleum. If we ran on a petroleum product, one glass a day would be enough. Much more convenient than six slices of bread and butter a day, two glasses of milk, and a meal of eggs, potatoes and vegetables, but not half as tasty! It would make us ill too; our bodies have a food engine not a petroleum engine. There are a lot of things we don't eat. Grass for one; we leave that to cows and goats. We leave worms to blackbirds and never dream of nibbling flies.

Every animal eats differently. Eagles eat weasels, weasels eat rabbits, rabbits eat plants. And plants? Plants hardly need to eat at all; the air keeps them alive. They get their energy from the sun. Thanks to the green pigment (chlorophyll) in their leaves, they absorb energy from the sun and store it in their tissues. When we eat a potato, we're actually using the energy which the plant had stored for itself. So when all is said and done, we run on the sun's energy. This even applies if we eat meat. Then we enjoy the sun's energy that the cow, sheep or pig has taken from the grass or from its feed. Later, when we're dead, we rot to dust and ashes, and these are useful, in turn, for the plants. These plants then provide food for animals which are eaten by human beings, and so on, round and round in a circle.

Theoretically, human beings can eat anything, plant or animal. But we don't. One person doesn't like yoghurt, another can't stand spinach. There's an even bigger difference between people from different countries. You get different food served in an Italian restaurant from that in a Chinese. In China they have all sorts of habits which we find really strange, like eating dog with fried jellyfish. In India, people won't touch beef because cows are considered holy. Muslims don't like the habit of eating pork, and the French think we'd be crazy for burying a pet rabbit instead of putting it in the pot. National customs are difficult to alter. Many people who are of Italian, Polish, Pakistani, Chinese and West Indian descent still eat as they always have done, even if their families have lived in a different country for years or generations. The British are no different. You still find Australians or Americans of British descent eating plum pudding in the blazing sun at Christmas, because that's what their grandparents always did. One of the only big new changes is to vegetarianism because people want to stop forests being felled for cows to graze. But even vegetarians keep the flavours of their cultures.

This reluctance of people to change their eating habits is fascinating for a researcher. Our clothes and furniture may become more and more artificial, but our food is still natural. Vegetables still grow, bread is still made from grain, meat and milk still come from animals. We no longer even have to hunt for our food; all we need to do is walk into the supermarket and buy it. And that's handy for us, because it means we don't have to go looking in the woods and fields for everything.

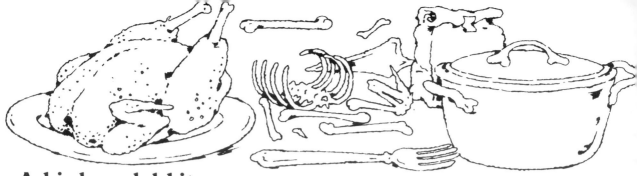

A bird model kit

It's a pity to throw away chicken bones because you think chickens are only good for eating. Next time you have chicken for dinner, keep all the bones. If you're a vegetarian, wait until you find a dead rabbit or other animal. Clean them and reconstruct the skeleton. You'll never want to make plastic model boats again. Animal skeletons have a better finish and the pieces fit together more snugly.

The best model kits are on sale in the supermarket among the poultry or walking around the woods. They're not in the toys and games sections of department stores. It's best when the chicken is boiled, but fried or roast ones are all right too. Chickens are usually sold without their heads but if you can find a farmer selling fresh chickens, not frozen, they'll give you the head if you ask. Collect all the bones. However clean the bones look, there'll still be some flesh on

them, so scrape these off with the sort of little knife you get in manicure sets and use an old toothbrush to get at the tender pieces underneath. Pins or an old-fashioned pen-nib are good for cleaning out the holes and cracks. The tendons (the tough white strings which hold small bones like ribs and vertebrae in place) can be left where they are.

Once the bones are clean, you'll need to remove the grease. To do this, put the bones in an old pan or pot containing household ammonia, cover with a lid to keep in the smell, and leave it for two days. Then take out the bones and rinse them under water. Now you can start fitting the bones together. First use a piece of wood and a length of wire to make a support for the pelvis (see below). Fix the legs and rib cage to it with glue and string. Tie the neck vertebrae and head to a second piece of wire and then fix them to the rear. Connect the head to the pelvis with a third piece of wire. Finally, put the skeleton out in the sun to bleach.

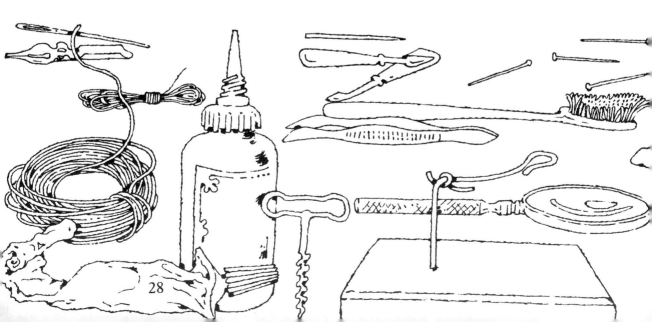

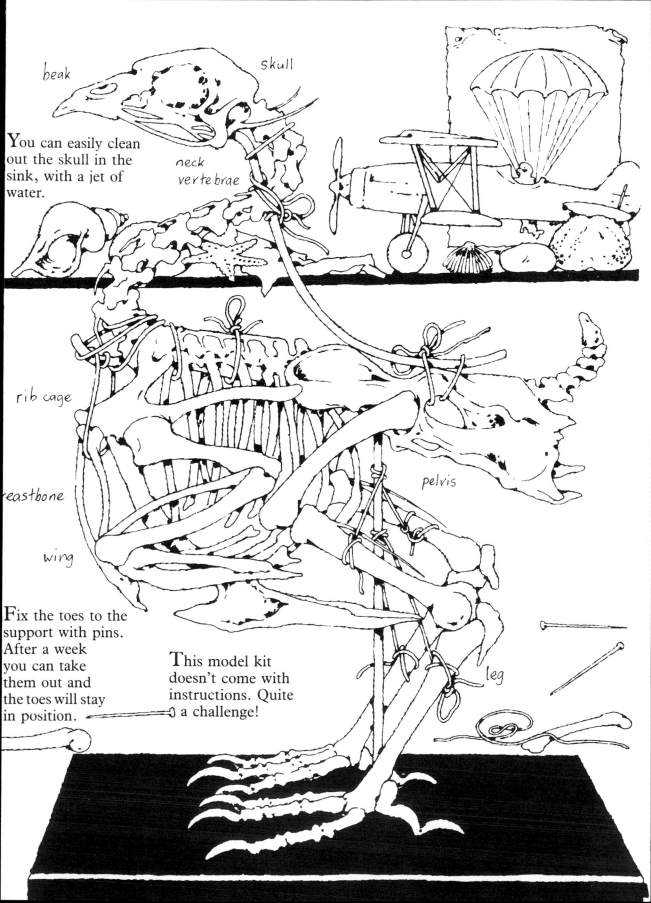

beak

skull

neck
vertebrae

You can easily clean
out the skull in the
sink, with a jet of
water.

rib cage

breastbone

wing

pelvis

Fix the toes to the
support with pins.
After a week
you can take
them out and
the toes will stay
in position.

This model kit
doesn't come with
instructions. Quite
a challenge!

leg

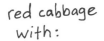

red cabbage with:

vinegar

water

soda water

Boil some red cabbage in water for half an hour. It'll turn blue and so will the water in the pan. Sieve the water and divide it equally between three glasses. Add white vinegar (an acid) to the first glass; it'll turn red. Add some water to the second and it'll stay blue, and add soda water to the last and it'll turn green. You could also try using another acid, like lemon juice, instead of vinegar.

Fun with vegetables

You can buy vegetables as well as flowers. The difference is that vegetables aren't there to look pretty; they're there to be eaten. Usually we only eat one part of a plant: the leaves of a lettuce, the fruit of a tomato plant, the seeds of a pea, the flower of a cauliflower. The other parts can sometimes even be poisonous; rhubarb leaves, for instance, can make you very ill indeed.

Fruit and vegetables don't die when you pick them. Sometimes you can even grow the whole plant again. Slice the top off a carrot (see below right), and put it in a deep saucer of water. A plant will shoot from it, and in time you'll be able to put it in a pot of earth. Save melon and green-pepper seeds. Wash them and leave them to dry for a couple of days before putting them in a pot of moist soil. You can plant orange and lemon seeds straightaway.

Onions are bulbs, just like tulips. Leave an onion in a warm, damp place and it'll start to sprout. Then put it in a pot, its green nose just under the damp soil. You'll get at least one flower from it, as beautiful as any tulip.

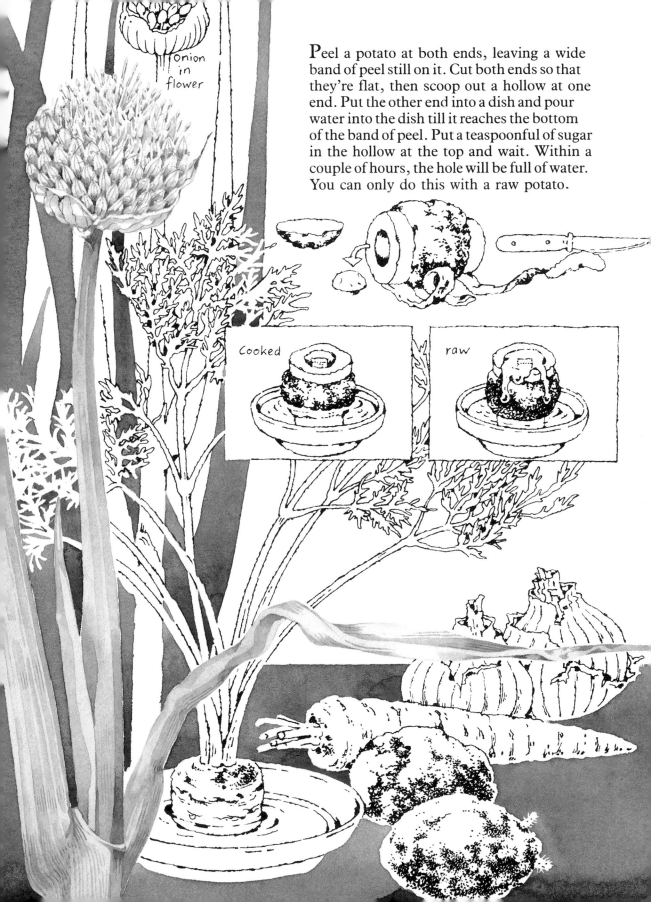

Onion
in
flower

Peel a potato at both ends, leaving a wide band of peel still on it. Cut both ends so that they're flat, then scoop out a hollow at one end. Put the other end into a dish and pour water into the dish till it reaches the bottom of the band of peel. Put a teaspoonful of sugar in the hollow at the top and wait. Within a couple of hours, the hole will be full of water. You can only do this with a raw potato.

Cooked

raw

Learn from a fish

If you want to know how a whole fish fits together, it's very easy to study. You could wait to find a dead fish. Or you could go to the fish market to take a good look at all the fish on display and buy one. Very often, fish are sold with head, tail and fins on, with only their guts taken out.

How do we know which parts of a fish are muscles? Because they're usually white or pink; animal muscle is red. Salmon and mackerel can be red, but that's because of the oil in them. If you want to be sure which is which, put a piece of fish and a piece of meat in warm place. Within an hour the fish will start to smell; meat will only stink after a day.

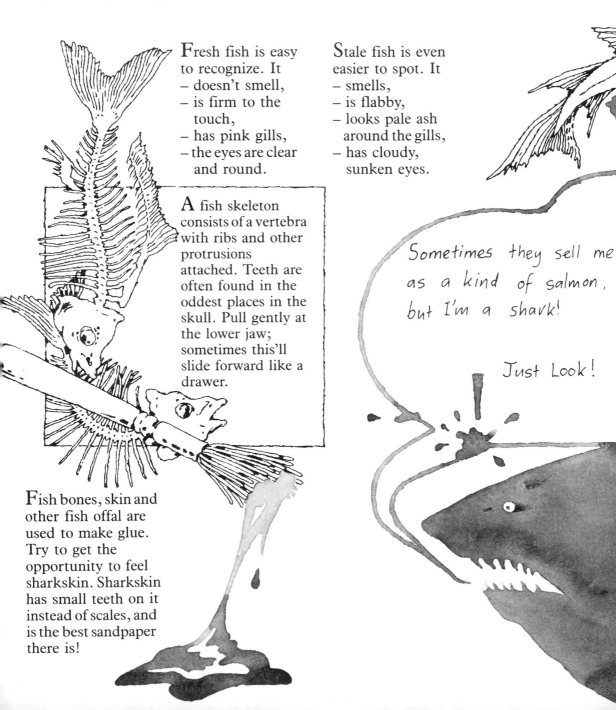

Fresh fish is easy to recognize. It
– doesn't smell,
– is firm to the touch,
– has pink gills,
– the eyes are clear and round.

Stale fish is even easier to spot. It
– smells,
– is flabby,
– looks pale ash around the gills,
– has cloudy, sunken eyes.

A fish skeleton consists of a vertebra with ribs and other protrusions attached. Teeth are often found in the oddest places in the skull. Pull gently at the lower jaw; sometimes this'll slide forward like a drawer.

Fish bones, skin and other fish offal are used to make glue. Try to get the opportunity to feel sharkskin. Sharkskin has small teeth on it instead of scales, and is the best sandpaper there is!

Sometimes they sell me as a kind of salmon, but I'm a shark!

Just Look!

Fish scales are splendid, especially when seen through a magnifying glass. Every type of fish has different types of scales. Dry them and stick them on to black cardboard.

Shark muscles are rather like pointed ice-cream cones the way they fit together.

Small sharks are usually sold without their skin and fins, but you can still recognize them from the slits where the fins used to be.

Help yourself

Animals in the wild don't have shops or farms. When they're hungry they just help themselves to what they can find in the surrounding countryside. It's all free. Unfortunately, the countryside no longer supplies all that we human beings like to have. Television and ice-cream do not grow on trees. Yet there's still a lot to be picked which is fun, or delicious, or both. But before you dash out you need to find out all about your local plants. Then, you'll be able to make fresh salads for your family. And you'll be able to make delicious real fruit yoghurts, herb teas, jams and summer drinks. There are also nuts and berries galore for you to gather and use.

Daisies and dandelions grow in grass. Make a hole in the daisy stems with your thumbnail and thread the stems through each other to make a daisy chain.
Pick dandelion leaves in spring when they are young, and add them to your cheese sandwich.
Delicious!

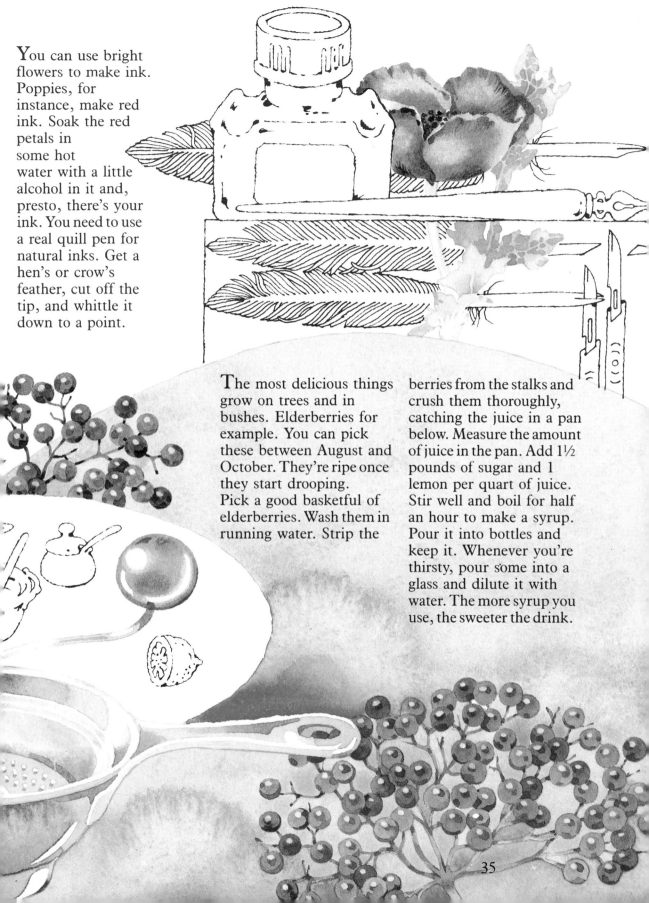

You can use bright flowers to make ink. Poppies, for instance, make red ink. Soak the red petals in some hot water with a little alcohol in it and, presto, there's your ink. You need to use a real quill pen for natural inks. Get a hen's or crow's feather, cut off the tip, and whittle it down to a point.

The most delicious things grow on trees and in bushes. Elderberries for example. You can pick these between August and October. They're ripe once they start drooping.
Pick a good basketful of elderberries. Wash them in running water. Strip the berries from the stalks and crush them thoroughly, catching the juice in a pan below. Measure the amount of juice in the pan. Add 1½ pounds of sugar and 1 lemon per quart of juice. Stir well and boil for half an hour to make a syrup. Pour it into bottles and keep it. Whenever you're thirsty, pour some into a glass and dilute it with water. The more syrup you use, the sweeter the drink.

35

PLANTS IN THE HOUSE

It's becoming more and more fashionable to have indoor potted plants at home, in restaurants and in offices. Most of them – geraniums, begonias and African violets – are different from outdoor plants, such as dandelions, roses and cowslips. Why don't we bring ordinary outdoor plants inside? Try it. Dig up a couple of common weeds from a field – first making sure there are plenty more where they came from – put them in a flower pot filled with soil and place them on the window sill. A blossoming clover will become a wilting bit of hay in no time at all. Outdoor plants would far rather be out of doors. So what's the big difference between inside and outside? Everything. Why else would people bother to build themselves houses? It's nice and dry inside, especially when the heat's on. Plants hate dry, heated rooms because they lose too much moisture in the dry atmosphere and they wither and droop (see p.66). You can prove that it's lack of water which is the main trouble by putting a large plastic bag loosely over a branch with green leaves. Fasten it under the branch. Drops of water will appear almost at once. The plants better suited to an indoor life are usually those which lose less moisture through evaporation, the sort of plants which are adapted for life in desert conditions. Cacti and succulents are two such varieties. You can recognize them by their thick leathery or prickly leaves.

It isn't just dry indoors, it's relatively dark too. This spells disaster for normal plants because they run on solar energy which they trap with their leaves. The only place they can do this is close to the window but unfortunately, the sun can shine so fiercely through the window that the leaves wither. Many house plants can survive a certain amount of darkness; those that come from woods, for example, where little light penetrates. Nevertheless, woods are damp, so the plants need to be sprinkled with water every day. The plant pot is another problem. In the natural state, a plant's roots spread out in all directions; in fact, a plant usually spreads as far below the soil as it does above it. Pots often cramp the plant's roots; they're rather like tightly fitting shoes. There may also be too little soil in the pot, which means that the plant will not absorb enough of the substances from the soil which it needs to grow. Good potting earth will go a long way, but even its goodness will be exhausted eventually. You could renew the soil, but it would be easier to pep up the soil already in the pot with manure or compost.

Many people complain about having to buy expensive soil for their indoor plants. Others feel so indignant, they rush out and dig up soil from their garden. Then, of course, the plants look ill and may even curl up and die. If the poor plant flourishes it will be because by pure chance it was dumped in exactly the one kind of soil that it really needed.

The people with real "green fingers" have either decided to blindly obey all the advice they read in a good plant book. Or they understand enough about the conditions and soil their special plants need. They know that you can't expect a plant that lived in a desert to survive in lovely rich rotting compost and a daily torrential downpour from an over-enthusiastic owner. Nor can you expect a tropical forest creeper to stand in dry desert soil above a central heating radiator. You could do your own experiment to see how many plants you can kill off! Choose cheap and easy plants which don't cost too much. (You can use outdoor bedding plants just as easily for this experiment.) Plant 4 or 5 healthy plants of each species in different kinds of soil. You can use dry soil from a building site, leafy forest loam, your own garden soil, acid soil from a garden store and the correct soil as advised by an expert or your local store. Some of your plants will look puny, stunted and sick – and others will grow miraculously. And if you have never before believed you had a way with plants, you will suddenly realise there is definitely hope for you.

There are more plants inside than you think, millions of them. They're spread all round the living room and the rest of the house, not only near the window sill and the light. They're so small that you can't see them and they haven't any green leaves so they don't need to trap the sun's energy. They live like animals, eating other plants or animals, living or dead. They're what we call bacteria and fungi. You can see them easily enough once they form a large enough mass but you need a magnifying glass or even a microscope to see them individually. When bacteria have had enough to eat, they split in two. Each half grows to full size and then in turn splits and you get four and the process is quickly repeated: 2, 4, 8, 16, 32, 64, 128, 256, 512, 1024 and so on until within one day there are too many to count and you've got a thick mass of them. Half of what we excrete is bacteria, coming out with the undigested remains of our food. They don't do us any harm. (There are only a few sorts of bacteria which make us ill).

Fungi reproduce themselves differently, with seeds called spores. The air's full of them. They'll float around for months if necessary, waiting for suitable food to land on. A stale slice of bread is a treat, especially if it's a bit moist, because, like all creatures, fungi need moisture. They like warmth too. The hotter it is, the faster they grow – the spores becoming filaments, the filaments becoming an enormous mass and the mass producing fruit bodies which make the new spores. Our body temperature is about the peak of pleasure for fungi; hotter than that and they die.

On the whole, people don't like the idea of fungi. Yet we use them (as yeast) in baking bread and brewing beer, and the important medicine penicillin is made from the fungus that grows on bread. Fungus is sometimes deliberately introduced to cheese, Roquefort for example. You can taste it too.

Pampering your house plants

People enjoy having plants around and they sometimes bring them inside in pots. Plants don't really like this. Houses are built for people. As far as plants are concerned, houses are too warm and dry, they have no bees to pollinate them, and they're smelly.

What's good for us can be bad for house plants. Fruit for example. Just the smell is too much for a plant, so never put plants next to a bowl of fruit on the window sill. Which fruit is the worst? Let's find out. Take three young plants – all the same variety – and put them under a glass cover (turn a large glass upside down, or a bowl or vase). Put a ripe apple inside the glass cover next to the first plant, leave the second one on its own and put a mandarin next to the third. Record in your log book how they grow. The first plant will grow most slowly, the second the fastest, and the third will be somewhere in between.

Plants, like people, can survive without food for weeks, but without water for only a few days. So water your plants often. But what should you do when you go on a trip? You could manage yourself, with the help of some tricks. Try these out before you go away.
– Put piles of wet newspaper in the bottom of the bath and put the plants, in earthenware pots, on top of the paper. As long as the bathroom gets daylight, the plants will survive for a long time.
– If your bathroom hasn't any windows, arrange the plants around a large jug of water. Link each plant to the jug with a length of wool or cotton. The wool sucks up the water and carries it to the plant. If you put the wool inside plastic tubing to stop water evaporating on the way, it'll be even better.
– Quench the plants' thirst with water from an empty wine bottle. Fill the bottle with water and push it into the soil upside-down. The pot will drink quickly at first, glug-glug-glug, but as soon as the soil is so wet that no more air can penetrate, this'll stop, and it'll drink more only when the soil has dried out a little. It's automatic!

begonia

Not much pollination or seed distribution goes on in the living room, so we need to help the plants reproduce. African violets are easy to begin with. Cut off a leaf, leaving a bit of stem. Put the stem into a pot of moist earth, and a new African violet will grow. You can do the same with peperomia, gloxinia and streptocarpus.

African violet

Grow the soles of your shoes

Either you buy plants or you're given them. What about the wild plants and flowers outside? Where do they come from? Plants appear on waste ground as if out of thin air, unless someone has sown them without anyone noticing. The wind and animals have sown them, and so have you and I.

Plants use us like messengers, without our even noticing. Their seeds and fruit cling to us and wait to be distributed. Some plants are better at this than others. Let's see which these are. We're going to grow some muddy soil.

If you want to know exactly which seeds you've picked up on your shoes, put down masking tape (the sort that goes round the edges of windowpanes before you paint the woodwork), sticky side up and then walk on it. The seeds will stick to it. Scrape them off and grow them.

Fill a shallow metal container with potting earth. Put it in a hot oven for a few minutes to kill off any tiny seeds which might be in the soil (so that the only seeds growing will be those you bring in). Let the soil cool. Now scrape the stuff off the soles of your shoes and rake it loosely into the top layer of soil. Water it, and set the container on the window sill in the sun. Tiny seedlings will quickly start shooting up. Once they grow into wild flowers, try to identify them. If you don't believe that they all come from the soles of your shoes, try doing this experiment with a plastic bag of soil from your garden shop.

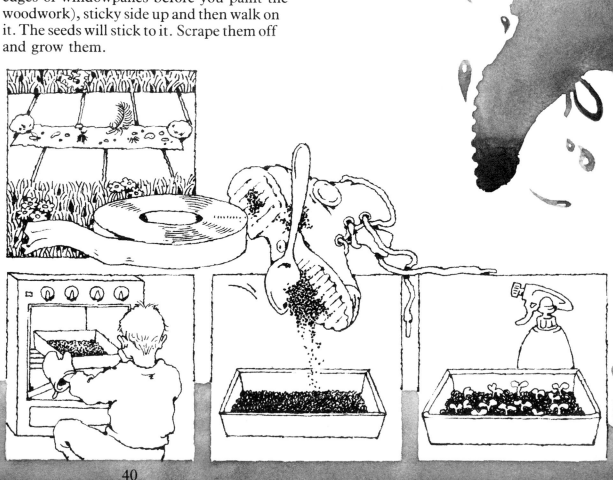

Plantain, buttercups, grass, thistle and daisies are just some of the wild plants you can grow from your shoes. Sometimes whole strands or seeds may cling to your clothes.

The seeds you pick up on the soles of your shoes depend on where you've been walking. Compare the harvest from a walk in the woods with what you grow from walking along the edge of a field. What about the town? Will a day's wandering through town produce anything for the window sill?

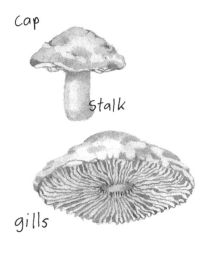

cap

stalk

gills

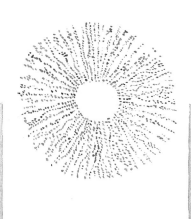

Let them go rotten

Plants and flowers adorn our window sills and our gardens. They're beautiful, which is why nurseries and garden shops do such a roaring business.
Yet people don't like rotten pieces of food or fungus and if they find it growing on bread or jam, they throw it away immediately. This is a pity because fungi are plants too, often just as lovely as the flowers from the nursery, provided you give them time to grow.

You can buy fungi at the supermarket. The most usual sort are mushrooms, which are actually the flowers of a fungus. Look for a ripe mushroom; it should look like an open umbrella underneath. We don't need the stalk for this experiment so twist it off at the top. Put the cap down on a piece of paper and cover it with a glass. Leave for a day. Then carefully remove the glass and the cap of the mushroom, and you'll see a fine image left behind on the paper. Hold your breath or you'll blow the powdery picture away. The powder is actually the spores, as the mushroom seeds are called, from underneath the cap. You can fix the picture by spraying it with hairspray, but hold the can at a good distance. Make spore figures from other sorts of mushrooms to get different patterns and shapes. Use black paper instead of white for toadstools with white spores.

When the fungus is magnified, you can see the spore cases, the fruit bodies, in which the spores are formed

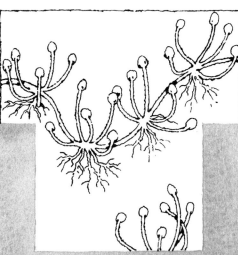

42

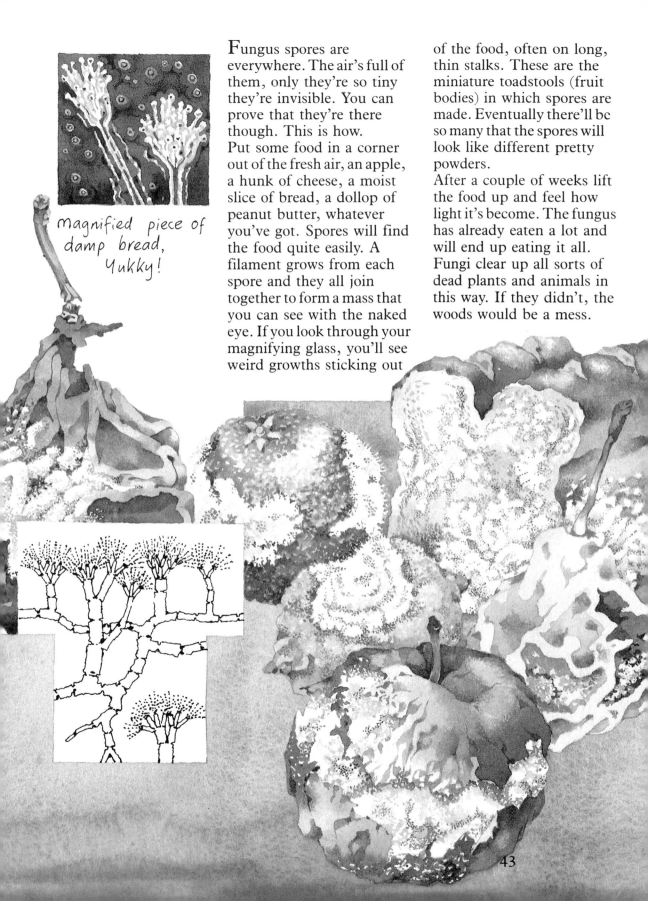

Fungus spores are everywhere. The air's full of them, only they're so tiny they're invisible. You can prove that they're there though. This is how.

Put some food in a corner out of the fresh air, an apple, a hunk of cheese, a moist slice of bread, a dollop of peanut butter, whatever you've got. Spores will find the food quite easily. A filament grows from each spore and they all join together to form a mass that you can see with the naked eye. If you look through your magnifying glass, you'll see weird growths sticking out of the food, often on long, thin stalks. These are the miniature toadstools (fruit bodies) in which spores are made. Eventually there'll be so many that the spores will look like different pretty powders.

After a couple of weeks lift the food up and feel how light it's become. The fungus has already eaten a lot and will end up eating it all. Fungi clear up all sorts of dead plants and animals in this way. If they didn't, the woods would be a mess.

magnified piece of damp bread, Yukky!

43

A seedy picture

Cress is the ideal plant. It's cheap, you can grow it on the window sill, it grows quickly, and you don't even need soil. It tastes good and you can do things with it. Your health food shop will recommend other little seeds to sprout if you can't find cress.

Sow cress or small seeds indoors in a shallow dish on a layer of kitchen paper towels. The seeds quickly produce stems and roots. Sprinkle the tiny plants every day with water. After about ten days, the stems should be 2 inches long. Cut them and put the cress in a sandwich, with egg or on its own, and perhaps with a squeeze of lemon. First though, let's do some experiments with the cress.

Let's see if cress likes warmth. Sow the seed in two dishes. Put one in a cool place and the other in the warmth. Every day note down in your log book the temperature in each place and the height of the plants. Where do they grow faster?

Grow your self-portrait in cress. Pin a sheet of drawing paper to the wall and ask a friend to draw round your head in pencil. Take the paper down from the wall and cut out the head. Throw the head away, and put the rest of the paper on top of a pile of kitchen paper towels in a dish. Sprinkle seed over the face shape and then take the drawing paper away. Sprinkle this dish with water. A week later, you'll be able to eat your own head. Yummy!

Cress is very useful for experiments because it grows so quickly. But other little edible seeds will all be fun too. (See drawing on the right).

1. Put an empty toilet paper roll on its end in a dish of cress and leave it there for a couple of days. You'll find when you lift it off that the cress inside the roll has grown more quickly than the cress outside the roll, though it won't look as healthy. The plants inside the roll needed to grow higher to reach the light and this used all their energy.

2. Put a dish of cress at a little distance from the window. Within a day, the plants will lean in the direction of the window. This is because the side of the stem closer to the light grows more slowly than the side away from it.

3. Roots grow towards moisture, not light. Sow some cress in a strainer lined with a shallow layer of peat, and wait for the roots to grow down through the strainer. Then hang it at an angle above a bowl of water. You'll see the tiny roots growing in the direction of the water as they react to the moisture in the air above it.

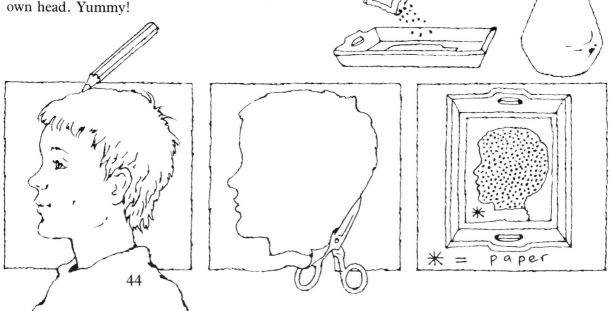

✳ = paper

44

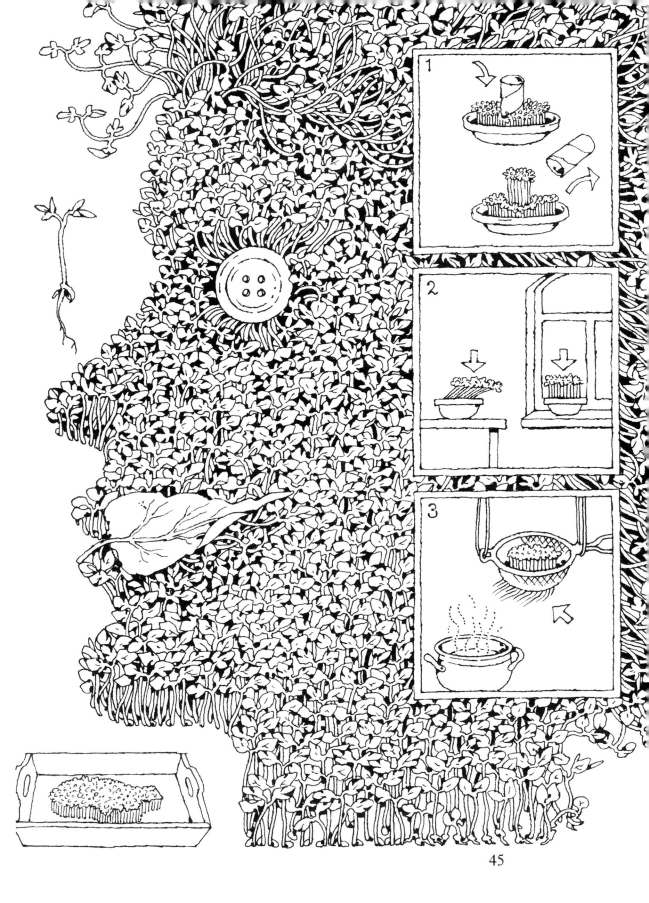

LOOKING FOR CLUES

A murder has been committed and the police are investigating. In a detective television series, there'd be wild chases with a lot of shooting and violence and dead bodies. Sherlock Holmes, the famous detective, would have handled it differently. He'd rather use his eyes than a gun. He had one hard and fast rule – that everyone and everything leaves clues behind. He looked for these clues, with a magnifying glass if need be: footprints, a hair, scorch marks left by bullets. Just by looking at a man's footprints, Sherlock Holmes could tell whether he was the culprit, how tall he was, where he had been going, whether or not he had been in a hurry, and if he'd been carrying anything. Had the knife entered the body at an upward angle from behind? Then the murderer must have been hiding behind the curtains. What sort of mud was in the footprint? Aha, river clay, so the culprit came from outside town. Sherlock Holmes first looked for clues by careful observation, then he deduced what might have happened, and, finally, he drew his conclusions. He could work out exactly what had happened, even though he hadn't been there.

Animals behave just like crooks sometimes. Either they put on disguises, camouflage themselves, so they're difficult to see, or else they live at night when you're asleep and take to their heels at the slightest sound you make as you approach. Nature films on television are always exciting, with plenty of animals all doing things. Yet when you go to the woods, the only animals you meet are dogs. Where have all the deer and rabbits gone? Are they employed by television? Of course not. They're hiding. If you want to get to know them, you'll have to go to work as Holmes did: observe, deduce, conclude. Become a nature detective.

Look for clues: a chewed pine cone, bits of skin or wool caught on barbed wire, the gnawed bark of a tree trunk, droppings. The animals resume their activity quite quickly after they've been disturbed. Grasshoppers give away their position with their chirping, a rustling in the undergrowth brings you on the trail of a snake. Learn from the animals. When a bird wants to bring a worm up to the surface, it stamps on the ground; we can do the same. Birds of prey spot their quarry from above; we can build a lookout in a tree (see p.78). Don't try to be quicker than animals because you'll seldom succeed; try to outwit them instead. Sometimes you may have the chance to solve a murder, just like Holmes. The victim could be a blackbird, lying half-eaten at the edge of the path. Who did it? Look at the feathers. If they're scattered around and are still whole, a bird of prey is the culprit. They tear out the large feathers, one by one, before plunging their sharp beaks into the flesh at the chest. Look at the edges of the wound; you can see the sharp beak marks. Animal predators usually start by eating the intestines, and again they give themselves away by the feathers, biting them off where they enter the skin. The victim won't stay there for long. If the eyes have been pecked out, you'll know that crows and gulls have come for the remains.

As far as Sherlock Holmes was concerned, no one was a stranger. He needed only to see someone to know where they came from, what work they did, and a lot more besides. He could tell by the way the person dressed, and by small things such as a calloused finger or a scratched ring. Try it yourself; it isn't difficult. Next time you're sitting in a train or a waiting room, try guessing what the person next to you does for a living. Listen carefully to their accent or dialect to find out where they come from. It's even more fun to play this game with animals. Look at an animal's teeth to find out what it eats. Carnivores – meat-eaters – have large pointed teeth for tearing; herbivores – plant-eaters – have flat teeth for grinding; insectivores – insect-eaters – have small pointed teeth. Omnivores – like us, who eat everything – have a mixture of teeth. Is the animal itself edible? You can tell by how bright it is. Insects like bees either taste horrid, or they sting; their vivid reds and yellows are a warning to birds and other insectivores.
You can tell by their eyes which animals are predators and which victims. The quarry, like deer, have eyes at the side which give them a wide range of vision to warn them of approaching enemies. Wolves and other predators have eyes set forward so that they can estimate the distance they have to spring. Look at the fins on a fish. If they're at the back, looking like the feathers on an arrow, you've got a predator which catapults itself at its prey. A pike, for example.

You can tell how deep sharks live in the sea by looking at their tail-fin. If, as in dogfish, the top is wider than the bottom, the fish has to swim deep down, i.e. it lives on the seabed.

Animals tell us about themselves in many other ways. The more you know about nature, the more you'll understand these signs and so learn even more. In this way animals will stop being strangers and become acquaintances, or even friends.

Tracking

Real trackers know which animals live in the woods without even catching sight of one. They keep their eyes open for footprints, hanks of hair, broken twigs, droppings, and other telltale marks. Noses and ears tell them the rest. Animals eat and excrete, they mate and fight, and all these things leave traces.

Tracking isn't difficult, as long as you use your eyes. You have to learn to read tracks, just as you once learned the alphabet. The quickest way is to sketch everything in your logbook, with the measurements written down alongside. It is easiest to find footprints in freshly fallen snow or along the muddy banks of rivers and ponds. They will tell you what sort of animal made the prints, where it was going, and how fast. The faster an animal moves, the wider the distance between the prints will be. Look at the vegetation to see which animal has been eating them. If blades of grass have been eaten straight across, it was a horse. Sheep and cows chew a jagged line because they don't have any upper teeth in front. Pine cones whose scales stick out sideways have been attacked by birds who peck out the seeds; mice and squirrels gnaw the scales right off till the cone is bald. If the ground is covered in broken snail shells, you're in the middle of thrush territory. The thrush smashes the shells against a stone or other hard object to get at the snail inside to eat. Indigestible food is regurgitated and discarded in the form of pellets (see pp. 50-51) or droppings. Herbivores leave small round droppings and if you examine these you'll find bits of stalks. Rabbits excrete droppings in great communal piles, preferably on high ground, in order to mark out their territory. Some droppings have bits of insects, such as beetle casings, still gleaming in them. Most predators' droppings are pointed at one end. In theory, dog droppings should be pointed too, though with modern food they are often mushy instead.

Moles leave the clearest signs of all. As these small underground animals dig their shallow tunnels beneath the surface of the soil, they throw up the excess earth every now and again, forming what we call mole-hills.

mouse

sheep

rabbit

chicken

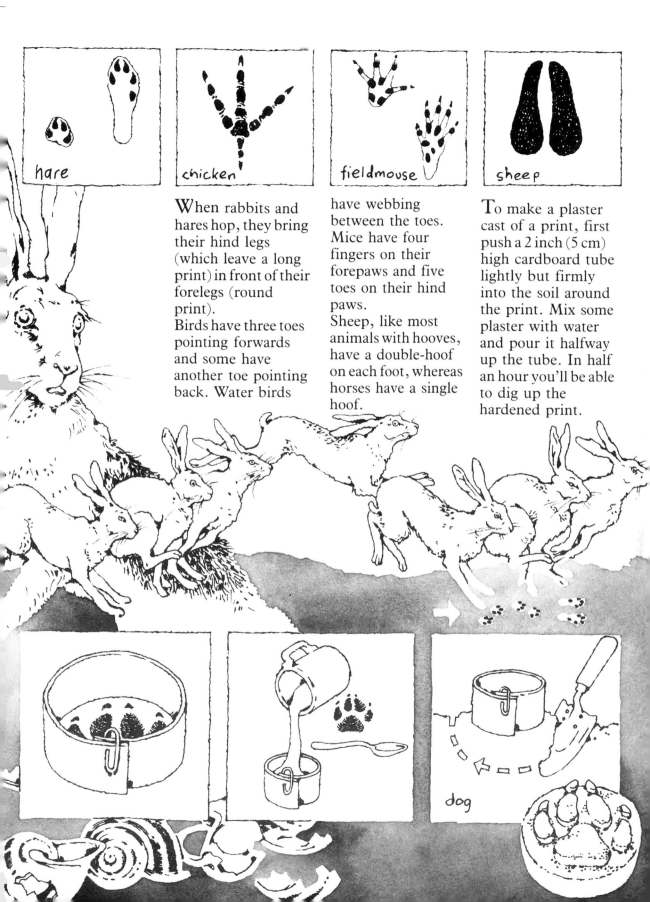

hare

chicken

fieldmouse

sheep

When rabbits and hares hop, they bring their hind legs (which leave a long print) in front of their forelegs (round print).

Birds have three toes pointing forwards and some have another toe pointing back. Water birds have webbing between the toes. Mice have four fingers on their forepaws and five toes on their hind paws.

Sheep, like most animals with hooves, have a double-hoof on each foot, whereas horses have a single hoof.

To make a plaster cast of a print, first push a 2 inch (5 cm) high cardboard tube lightly but firmly into the soil around the print. Mix some plaster with water and pour it halfway up the tube. In half an hour you'll be able to dig up the hardened print.

dog

Looking at owl pellets

You've probably been spattered by bird-droppings more than once, and you'll know all about the awful mess it leaves on your clothes! This is because bird droppings contain urine; birds excrete liquids and solids from the same hole. Owls have a second way of getting rid of undigested foods, by vomiting, or regurgitating. This vomit is clean and dry, and well worth investigating.

The mouth is a useful secondary excretory organ for owls because they eat their prey whole, skin, bones, beetle casings and all. The indigestible parts stay in the owl's stomach and once enough have accumulated, the owl regurgitates the lot in a ball, a pellet. You may sometimes find heaps of owl pellets below the place where the owl sleeps during the day: large balls for large owls, small balls for small owls.

By looking at the contents of an owl pellet you can find out exactly what an owl has eaten. You'll need tweezers and pins, and your eyeglass will come in handy here, too. Sometimes the hairs and feathers will have dried out so much that you won't be able to retrieve the little bones without damaging them. If this is the case, soak the pellet first in hot water. Remove the hairs and feathers which come to the surface, and change the water. Sort out bones and bits of insects according to type, and stick them on to a dark piece of cardboard. Use a fresh piece of cardboard for each pellet and write on the cardboard where and when you found it. If the pellet contains hairs and feathers but no bones, then it's been vomitted by another bird of prey, such as a falcon or hawk. Whereas owls hunt at night, these birds of prey hunt in the daytime, but unlike owls, the acid of their stomachs dissolves their victims' bones till nothing is left. If you find pellets with remains of plants in them, then they're from a crow or a gull.

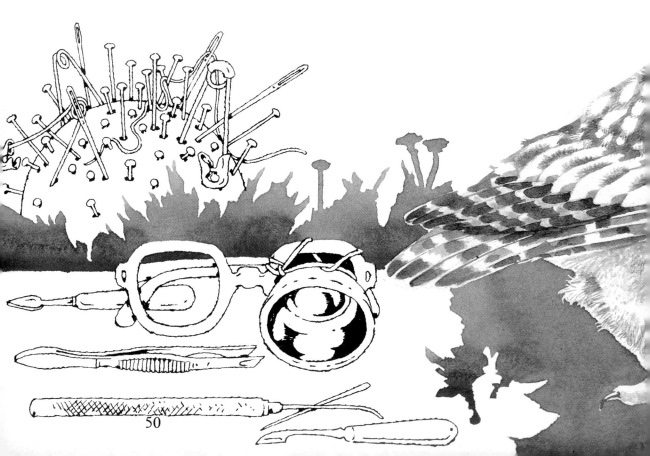

50

Bird and mice skulls (1 and 3 respectively) are easy to spot among the bones in an owl pellet. Ordinary mice have irregular teeth like ours (2), voles have high molars (4). Shrews' teeth are pointed. Apart from skulls, you'll find ribs, vertebrae, shoulder-blades, pelvises, paw-bones and wing bones. You'll also find the hard outer casing of insects. If the owl pellet is black, it probably came from the small barn-owl.

51

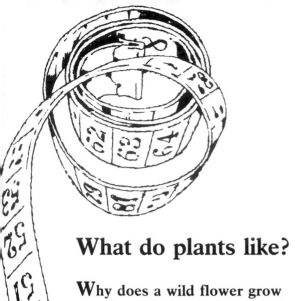

What do plants like?

Why does a wild flower grow exactly where it does instead of a little further along? To find out, all we need is a tape measure and a sharp mind.

There are thousands of different varieties of plants in our country, each of which has a place where it prefers to grow. Rushes like the edges of rivers, daisies like fields and lawns. There are good reasons for this. Rushes like water but need soil to germinate, so they grow between the land and the water. Every plant has some preference or other. One likes moisture, another can't stand shade, another likes to be high up. You can't always tell what these preferences are, so we're going to approach the matter scientifically by taking a cross-section of plants.

Put two sticks firmly in the ground, and stretch a tape measure between them in a straight line. In your logbook note down which plants the tape passes, and at what point. For example, one foot, (30 cms), feverfew. Mark down the height of the plant too. Look up the names of the plants in a flower guide book and if there are some you can't identify, put a question mark. Leave the sticks where they are when you've finished, so that you can repeat the process later in summer to see what the changes are.

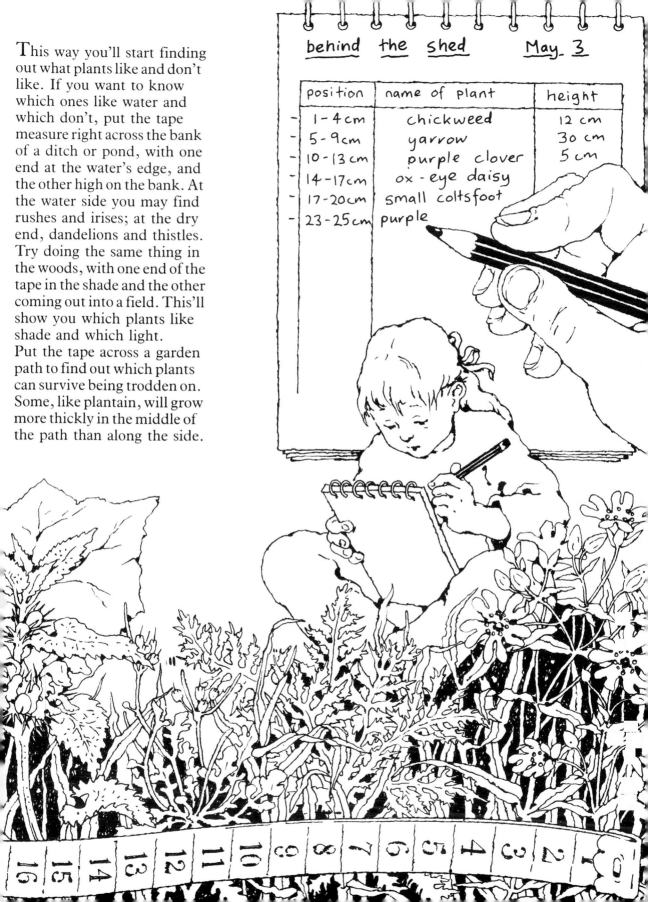

This way you'll start finding out what plants like and don't like. If you want to know which ones like water and which don't, put the tape measure right across the bank of a ditch or pond, with one end at the water's edge, and the other high on the bank. At the water side you may find rushes and irises; at the dry end, dandelions and thistles. Try doing the same thing in the woods, with one end of the tape in the shade and the other coming out into a field. This'll show you which plants like shade and which light.

Put the tape across a garden path to find out which plants can survive being trodden on. Some, like plantain, will grow more thickly in the middle of the path than along the side.

behind the shed   May 3

position	name of plant	height
1 - 4 cm	chickweed	12 cm
5 - 9 cm	yarrow	30 cm
10 - 13 cm	purple clover	5 cm
14 - 17 cm	ox - eye daisy	
17 - 20 cm	small coltsfoot	
23 - 25 cm	purple	

Bird-watching

Use a bird guidebook to look up the birds you see around you. Half the time you won't be able to see them. So listen carefully. Once you get to know a bird's song, you'll be able to say which bird is singing without even looking up.

Some bird-watchers know all there is to know about kingfishers, but precious little about sparrows or chickens, which is a pity. After all, chickens are birds too, even though they don't fly away as you watch them.

Chickens can be seen with the naked eye, but its useful to have binoculars for most other birds. The greater the magnification, the more the bird will fill the lens.

Chickens have an odd lurching sort of walk. They only have two feet and when they lift one, they're in danger of losing balance and falling over. This is why they hold the other foot at an angle, and move their head, as if it's tied to the foot with string. When the chicken's head is forward, where are its legs? And when the head is back? Draw both positions. Draw the chicken when it's scratching for food too, and when it's scratching itself. Chickens peck each other. There's one chicken at the top of the social scale or pecking order, which isn't pecked by any other chicken. It pecks the one below, that one the next, and so on down the scale.

Play a recording outside of a robin singing. If there's a real robin close by, it'll sing back. (The same happens with dogs. Record a barking dog, play it back, and you'll have all the dogs in the area in an uproar!) You can imitate the hoot of an owl. Fold your hands the way the girl in the picture is doing, put your lips to the knuckles of your thumbs and blow into the gap underneath. With some practice, you'll make an 'oo-hoo' sound and if there's an owl around it'll react to the sound.

Cut out twenty pieces of paper 3 x 2 inches (7 x 4 cm). On each one draw a chicken pecking. In the first ten draw the beak getting gradually higher and higher, and getting lower and lower again on the last ten. Put the sheets together in order and staple them on the left to make a small booklet. Hold the spine in your left hand and ruffle through the pages with your right, and the chicken pecks away like mad.

ANIMALS AT HOME

Cars have only been around for a hundred years. How did people manage before? What did they use for transport? What did they talk about? What did they wash at the weekend? The answer is, the horse. Many people went to work on horseback or went on journeys in carriages and carts pulled by horses. Wars were won and lost with horses; eight million died in the First World War alone.

Horses weren't the only animals in the service of man. Animals were used for a variety of purposes for which we now use machines. Geese were used as burglar alarms, pigs ate the left-overs, roosters woke people up, goats mowed the grass. Dogs were the most useful, and still are: they could stand guard, pull, hunt, rescue people, search for truffles, lead the blind, herd sheep.

All these important animals orginally slept in the house with their owners although later they were given their own quarters. This is why horses and geese are still called domestic animals. But not all creatures in the home are domestic animals. True domestic animals are tame and depend on humans; at the most, only twenty-five of the millions of different sorts of animals in the world are domestic. The best known are dogs, cats, cows, chickens, pigs, horses, donkeys, goats, sheep, rabbits, guinea-pigs and mice. Ten thousand years ago none of these existed. Since then, people have coaxed them away from their wild ancestors. We got tired of having to go to the forest to hunt every time we needed meat. So we started catching animals and keeping them alive until they bred. As the generations passed, so the animals grew tamer, until they became dependent on people for food and shelter. Their bodies changed too as they were bred for the qualities we needed. Cows' udders became larger and sheeps' fleeces woollier. Because the animals no longer had to think about hunting for food, their brains shrank in size and their intestines lengthened.

Now that there are tractors and combine harvesters, horses rarely have to pull carts any more. You might think they'd be pleased, but nowadays many horses kept in riding stables do no more than walk round and round the same boring circle, and most pigs are shut up in factory farm buildings without daylight where they gnaw each others' tails with frustation. Hens are often put together in impossibly small cages to lay eggs or be slaughtered when they're six weeks old. Animal protection societies have their hands full. Dogs and cats have surely got off more lightly. Nowadays they're hardly ever expected to pull carts or catch rats, except on some farms. All they have to do is be adorable, to recline on soft cushions and eat the flesh of their unluckier fellow animals in return for allowing themselves to be petted. But are they happy? That depends.

When dogs still had to work, different breeds had different jobs. Corgis herded cows, sheepdogs looked after sheep (as they still do), dachshunds went down rabbit-holes, retrievers retrieved birds. Because they are small, dachshunds are frequently kept as pets in city apartments nowadays, but what their owners don't realize is that the long climb up long flights of stairs can easily break their sausage-shaped backs. The snob appeal of owning a pedigree dog results in inbreeding and subsequent physical weaknesses. Huge dogs become too heavy for their legs and tiny dogs have so little room left in their heads for eyes that these bulge forward, blocking up their noses. Some chic cats have such long hair that they aren't allowed on the streets for fear of the beast getting its hair tangled up in something. If you love animals, take a mongrel, the healthiest 'breed' there is. More than a third of families own a dog or a cat. Some people think this is too many, particularly when they're awakened at night by cats fighting, or the birds in their gardens are eaten, or they see dogs fouling the streets and parks. These killjoys have quite a point; if we all loved each other more, would we need so many pets? There is a huge threat to nature all over our world. For instance, it takes five times as many fields to grow meat as it does to grow the same amount of vegetable protein. Because of this, many nature lovers are trying to cut down on meat. Dogs and cats also eat meat which puts more pressure on our already dwindling forests and wild life. For the sake of our trees and wilderness areas, perhaps all of us animal-lovers could keep to just one pet.

Nevertheless it is our pets that often teach us to love animals and we go on to love and protect other kinds of animals. And it's pets that teach us too. Biologists are always peering at rare birds through their binoculars, hardly sparing a thought for the dogs barking at their heels, or the cat rubbing against their legs. They should have close-up binoculars instead! Good contact with a dog or cat can teach us a lot about the mysteries of the animal kingdom.

Keep them small

Why should we only have a dog or cat or hamster as a pet? Keep butterflies instead, or wasps or ants!

It's amazing to think that such a splendidly delicate creature as a butterfly was once a fat crawling caterpillar. Perhaps we should see the transformation or metamorphosis for ourselves. Put a large jar on its side and line the bottom with newspapers. Look for caterpillars among the cabbages and put them into the jar. Give them fresh cabbage leaves every day. Clear away any old uneaten leaves and stalks by sliding out the top layer of newspaper. Weigh the fresh leaves you put in and the remains you bring out and compare the two. The difference is how much caterpillars need to eat before they pupate and become a butterfly, and when you've seen the beautiful butterfly emerge, it's time to let it fly free.
Sometimes wasps lay eggs inside chrysalids. The young wasp hatches and eats up the caterpillar. Then, instead of a butterfly, a wasp emerges. Other wasps lay their eggs on the leaves of trees and the leaf forms a hollow ball, called a gall, around the eggs. If you want to find out what this kind of wasp looks like, put a gall into a cardboard box and stick a bottle into the side. When the wasp hatches, it'll fly into the bottle looking for light, and you'll be able to see it.

You can make your own ant colony. Find a column of ants and if they disappear under a brick or loose paving stone lift it up, quickly scoop them up with a spoon, and put them into a plastic bag. Take some pupae (they look like grains of rice) too. The queen is the most important. You'll recognize her immediately because she's the largest ant and is constantly surrounded by workers (ordinary ants). She is the only one who can lay eggs and guarantee the continuation of the ant colony. When you get inside, attach the plastic bag to the tube. Provided the plaster is slightly damp and you have covered the nest with some dark material, the ants will walk in quite happily. Once they are in, you can feed them by putting pieces of meat or fruit, jam and honey into a jar and attaching that to the tube. Before you know it, they'll have settled in; larvae here, pupae there, food somewhere else.
Now you can carry out experiments. What happens if you put a live beetle in the bottle, or a strange ant? What do the workers do about their queen?

58

To make the ants' home, you'll need a glass plate 12 inches x 16 inches (30 x 40 cm). (1). Model ranges of hills on it in clay (2), and block them off with a piece of wood at one end (3). Build a wooden frame round the plate (4), as in the picture. It should finish parallel with the glass at the end opposite to the block of wood (5) and be 1 cm. wider than wood (3). Pour plaster of Paris into the frame, wait for it to harden, turn the whole thing upside down, remove <u>all</u> the wood and clay, and you're left with a plaster ants' colony with passages (8), feeding trough (9), feeding tube (7), and sliding roof (10). When you're not watching the colony, cover it with some dark material.

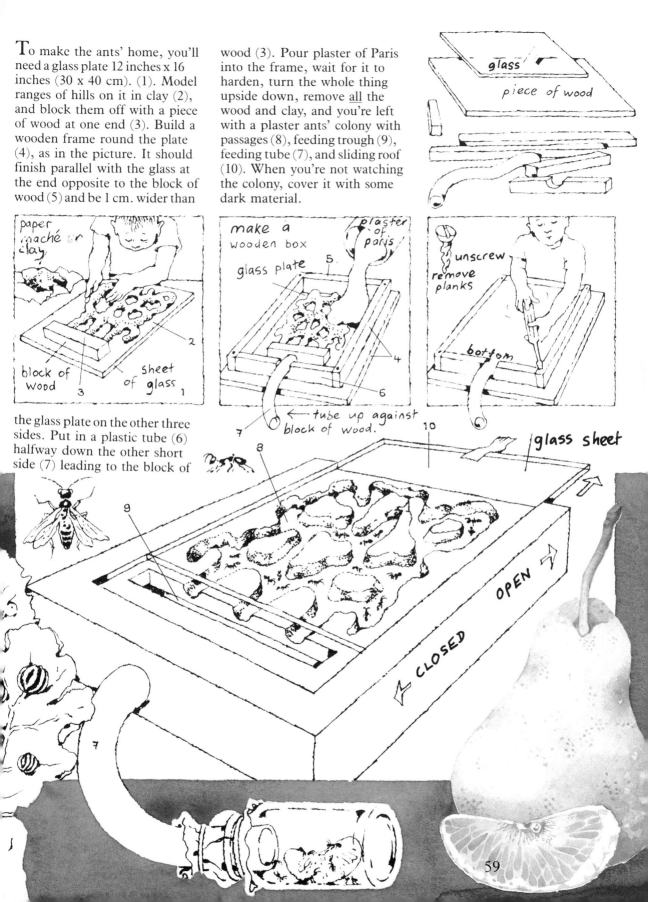

glass

piece of wood

paper maché or clay

block of wood

sheet of glass

3

2

1

make a wooden box

glass plate

plaster of paris

5

4

6

7 ← tube up against block of wood.

unscrew remove planks

bottom

the glass plate on the other three sides. Put in a plastic tube (6) halfway down the other short side (7) leading to the block of

8

9

10

glass sheet

OPEN

CLOSED

7

Cat-watching

You needn't go all the way to Africa to watch animals hunt. There's one right under your nose. The cat may be tame when lying quietly on your lap, but once he's outside with the other cats he's as wild as they come. As far as he's concerned, your backyard is a jungle. Think of it that way yourself and observe cats as if they were lions in Africa. Watch them closely, and write down everything you see.

Start by getting to know all the cats in your street. Every one is different. Make a sketch of each one, paying particular attention to size, patches and stripes, so that you can distinguish between them. Give it a name which fits its description, like Redbeard or Tiger, or Sooty or Coal if it's a black cat. Next to the sketch write down everything you can find out about the cat: male or female, owner's address, and so on.

Cats follow a regular pattern throughout the day, so regular it sometimes seems as if they can tell the time! Every day for a week write down what time your cat (or your friend's) goes to sleep, wakes up, goes out and wants to be let in again. Make a note of the time the local cats appear at certain vantage points, hunt and leave again. Does this follow a pattern too?

Observe the local cats from the same place each day and at the same time. Note down what you see. Who fights whom? Who wins? Who avoids whom? Which cats are friends? Are tomcats more aggressive than females? Does a cat behave differently on its own territory than on strange ground, and if so, how? Try to find out which cat is boss. It's usually a powerful looking tomcat who rarely fights but seldom loses when he does: he walks high on his paws.

Cats lapping milk do not swallow with every lap. How many laps does your cat take before swallowing?

Taming wolves

There have always been cats. But there were no dogs until man tamed the wolves, centuries ago.

Wolves are social animals, hunting in packs. Dogs inherited this social instinct; when they see another dog in the street they always want to play.

A cat is quite different. She'll catch her own bird, thank you. Strange cats just mean competition for food and she chases them away.

It isn't easy weighing dogs and cats because they won't stay still. The best thing to do is weigh them with you, then weigh yourself; subtract your own weight from your joint weights and you'll know how heavy the animal is.

Weigh your cat or dog, then give them a whole can of pet food to eat and weigh them again straight after. Has their weight really gone up more than the weight given on the label?

Tall people are bothered more by heat than short people are, and they sweat more. Dogs are bigger than cats and they have the same problem. When they get hot they soon begin to sweat (through their tongues, not their foreheads like us) and pant. See what temperature it is and record how often the dog pants in a minute. Repeat when it gets hotter. Is the dog panting faster?

Male dogs urinate more often than they seem to need to. Why don't they just make one big puddle? Because they want other dogs to know which lamppost is theirs. The other dogs smell that and come and urinate against it too.
Draw a map of your local area. Every time you take out the dog, put a cross where it urinates. Does it usually go to the same places? Do other dogs go there too?

Some people have their dogs' tails docked or lopped off. This is as bad as cutting out peoples' tongues, because dogs "talk" with their tails. One dog phrase you're sure to know is the simple wag, meaning "I'm happy." There are other phrases too. In the four pictures below, the dog's saying, "I don't really like what you're doing" (1); "everything's fine" (2); "I submit" (3); and "I don't know." (4).

These dogs have their teeth bared threateningly. The dog on the right is more dangerous than the one on the left. This is because it feels cornered, as you can tell by its wrinkled-up nose.

A pond inside

Most aquariums have small tropical fish swimming round and round, their environment controlled by pumps, filters, lamps and heating devices. It's very pretty, like a live painting, but if you really want to experience something, you'll find it's more fun making a pond-aquarium.

Catch some creatures from a pond and put them in a large jar; add a dash of Canadian pondweed and your pond-aquarium is ready. Put the pot near the window, but out of the full glare of the sun. Water beetles hang from the surface of the water to breathe, leeches twist and turn in search of prey, spiders build diving-bells, snails graze off the algae on the glass; it's a hive of activity. Give them tubifex, water fleas and other aquarium food to eat. Some creatures will eat each other, but they do that in ponds too. It's all part of the famous balance of nature.

Nothing can be more beautiful for an aquarium than sticklebacks in spring. Try catching a male first; at this time of year he's every bit as beautiful as a tropical fish. Put him in a bowl with a layer of sand on the bottom, a dash of Canadian pondweed and some algae. He'll use these to build a nest, adding glue from his own body. If you put in another male he'll chase the stranger relentlessly. It's better to put in a female (1), her belly swollen with eggs, and watch the male do a zig-zag dance around her (2). If she reacts by taking up a certain position (3), he'll nudge her and show her the nest (4). Eventually she'll go to it (5) to lay her eggs (6) which the male then fertilizes (7). The male does the rest, so now you can take out the female and let her free. He waves fresh water over the eggs and takes care of the tiny fish when they emerge. If they wander too far from the nest, he catches them in his mouth and spits them back into the nest.

Unlike fish, insects don't have gills, so they need to swim up to the surface for air, which they carry back down like a silver bell. How do they know where the surface is? Usually because of the light. We can demonstrate this by putting water-beetles into a jar, covering up the top to make it dark and putting a light underneath. The beetles will swim to the bottom of the jar to try to get air; and you'll see backswimmers, called that because they swim on their backs, swimming the "right" way up for once!

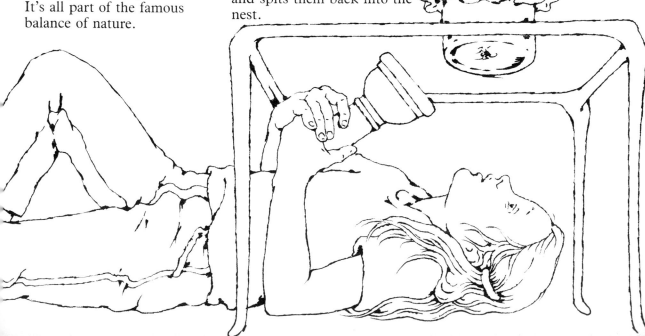

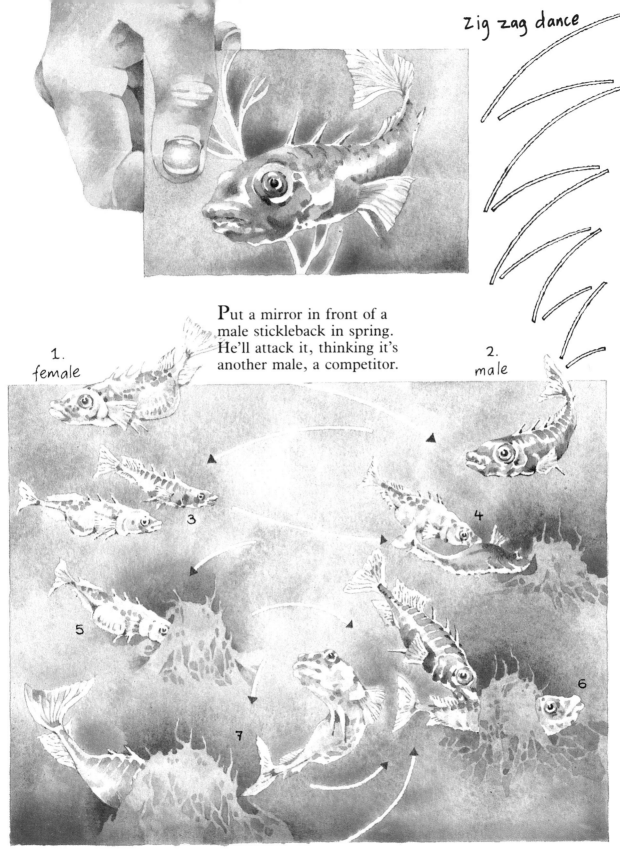

Zig zag dance

Put a mirror in front of a male stickleback in spring. He'll attack it, thinking it's another male, a competitor.

1. female

2. male

3

4

5

6

7

MYSTERIOUS FORCES

You can play tricks with life. In the following pages, we get an egg to drink, a stalk to curl up, and peas to roll. None of these tricks is difficult; in fact, everything only does what comes naturally. You just have to summon up their mysterious forces. We don't always know how these work, but work they do. The tricks on the following pages are mainly based on two forces, suction and growth.

Everything living drinks water. Our whole body cries out for it. Thirst is worse than hunger. You can stay alive for more than a year without food – at any rate, someone did in 1966 – but you can usually go only a couple of days without drinking. The record was set by a boy buried in rubble who went for 252 hours, just over ten days, without drink. Our bodies need water, which is hardly surprising, since we are two-thirds water, and babies as much as ninety per cent. That percentage falls to sixty when you grow old and dry out, which is why old people have wrinkles. By the end of your life, you'll have used up 50,000 pints of water through urination, sweat, exhalation and evaporation. All we can do is keep topping up the water level so that it does not fall below the halfway mark. If it does, we die. Animals are no different. A woodlouse was originally a water creature (see p.75). They actually have tiny gills, and in fact the rest of their family, shrimps and crabs, still live in water. In order to survive, a woodlouse always looks for damp places. They carry the eggs in a brood pouch filled with liquid, under their belly.

Plants need water even more. They have no bones and only stay upright by sucking up so much water that it keeps them stiff. Without it, they wilt. Why can't you prick them and make them leak? Because they're made up of millions of tiny watertight compartments called cells. Cook a stalk of celery and the cell walls will break down, releasing the juice, and what was once so firm, becomes soft.

Plants suck up their water through their roots. How? Surely they don't have a pump? No, the suction power of the roots is based on another mysterious force, osmosis. Water is sucked up, or absorbed, from a solution through a membrane which lets the water through but not what has dissolved in it. The skin of a carrot is a membrane, for instance, and the juices inside the vegetable the solution. Osmosis can be demonstrated with an egg (see p.71). The skin just under the shell is the membrane, and the white and yolk are the solution. In the potato test on p.31, each cell was a separate compartment. Once the potato was cooked, the cells broke down and could no longer suck.

Peas and other seeds can absorb water even though they don't have roots. They can put on quite a show! Fill a bottle with dried peas, top it up with water and close it tightly. Put the bottle in a safe place and cover it with a cloth. Within a day, the glass will break because of the force of the peas swelling.

Growth is as powerful a force as suction. If you get fatter, the buttons will tear off your shirt! Don't underestimate the growing force of a young plant. Grass may look tender, yet it can shoot up through asphalt. You can demonstrate this force with any fast growing seed. Sow some cress (see p.44) and cover it with a transparent plastic folder. The cress will actually lift the folder up as it grows. Put coins or other small weights on the file and see whether the tiny plants continue growing.

Lovers sometimes carve their initials in a heart on a tree-trunk. Twenty-five years later the tree will have grown, so how much higher up the trunk will the heart have moved? A little higher? Right to the top? It'll still be at the height from the ground where it was carved. This is because trees are plants, and plants usually grow from the tips of their branches. Think of a tree like a tower of bricks which keeps being added to at the top.

Trees grow until they die; human beings stop growing after about twenty, although some parts of us, like nails, never stop. How fast do your nails grow? Scratch one near the cuticle and see how many days it takes for the mark to reach your fingertip. Brains stop growing even earlier, when we're twelve. It's reached adult size by then. So you should in fact be at your sharpest when you're twelve! And because young brains are so strong, adults send you to school to cram them with as much learning as possible. It's as well that you've got secret powers, or your head would have burst long ago!

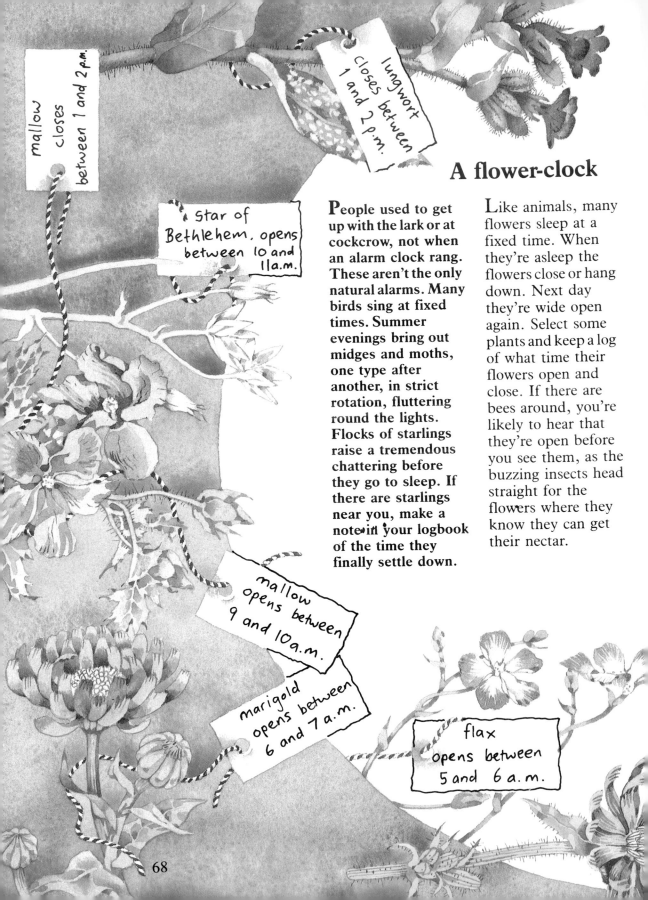

mallow closes between 1 and 2 p.m.

lungwort closes between 1 and 2 p.m.

Star of Bethlehem, opens between 10 and 11 a.m.

A flower-clock

People used to get up with the lark or at cockcrow, not when an alarm clock rang. These aren't the only natural alarms. Many birds sing at fixed times. Summer evenings bring out midges and moths, one type after another, in strict rotation, fluttering round the lights. Flocks of starlings raise a tremendous chattering before they go to sleep. If there are starlings near you, make a note in your logbook of the time they finally settle down.

Like animals, many flowers sleep at a fixed time. When they're asleep the flowers close or hang down. Next day they're wide open again. Select some plants and keep a log of what time their flowers open and close. If there are bees around, you're likely to hear that they're open before you see them, as the buzzing insects head straight for the flowers where they know they can get their nectar.

mallow opens between 9 and 10 a.m.

marigold opens between 6 and 7 a.m.

flax opens between 5 and 6 a.m.

morning glory
closes
between 4
and 5 p.m.

Some flowers are so punctual that you can use them to make a clock. Each of the twelve digits on the clock face will be a different kind of flower, opening or closing or smelling most sweetly at the hour it represents. We have chosen twelve flowers, but in your area some may close or open earlier or later than ours, so you might like to find a flower yourself which works better.

How does a flower open and close? It doesn't have muscles, does it? Tulips tell us the answer. They work according to temperature, opening in warmth, closing in cold. Put a tulip in a vase and move it around from a warm place to a cold and back a couple of times. Wait till the petals are completely open or closed and measure how long they are. They're growing! When it's warm, petals grow mainly on the inside so that they can spread out; in the cold they do just the opposite so that the flower can close.

evening primrose
opens
between 5
and 6 p.m.

marvel of Peru
opens between
6. and 7 p.m.

geranium
smells strongest
about 8 p.m.

chicory
opens between
4 and 5 a.m.

69

The egg test

At the moment that a chicken lays an egg, the young chick inside is as tiny as the head of a pin. The rest of the egg is stuffed full of food, egg white and yolk to feed the chick to make it grow. People usually get there before the chicks, either by eating the eggs or by using them for experiments.

Eggshell is made of calcium which makes it hard yet fragile. When the chicken pushes it out of her body the egg is still soft; it hardens once it comes in contact with the air outside. We're going to make the shell soft again. First we need to find a bottle whose neck is just too narrow for the egg to pass through. Put the egg in a bowl of vinegar for a day and night. Vinegar is an acid which dissolves calcium and so softens the shell. Now you'll be able to get the egg inside the bottle.

There are thousands of holes in the shell of an egg, so tiny that you can hardly see them. They're there so that the chick inside can breathe. You can prove that there are holes by boiling the egg. Put it in a pan of cold water. Quite soon you'll see masses of little air bubbles rise to the surface. Put an egg among some onions, or next to washing powder for a couple of days. Then boil it and eat it. It'll taste of onions or of freshly laundered clothes because their smell will have penetrated the egg through the holes along with the air. Can you tell if an egg has already been boiled? Put one on a plate and spin it. Stop it with your finger by touching it very briefly. A boiled egg will stop spinning at once; a raw egg will carry on. This is because in a raw egg the yolk works just like the flywheel of a toy car which continues to revolve long after you've set it going.

Many people prick a hole in their egg to stop it cracking while it boils. In theory they're right to do this; the only trouble is that they

often prick it the wrong way, at the pointed end instead of the blunt, and that's no use because the hollow air chamber is at the blunt end. When you prick the blunt end, air can escape (watch the bubbles when you cook it) and the egg stays whole.

For our last egg experiment, prick a hole in both ends of a raw egg. Carefully break off bits of shell around the hole at the blunt end, and you'll be able to look inside the air chamber. (Make sure that you don't break the inner membrane when you prick the shell.) Put the egg, blunt side down, in a glass of water, so that the pointed end sticks out just above the water. The egg can't leak from the bottom because of the inner membrane – but it can from the top! After half an hour a sort of mucous ball comes out of the top hole. What has happened? The egg has sucked up water from underneath, absorbed it through the membrane, and then the water has pushed the contents of the egg up and out.

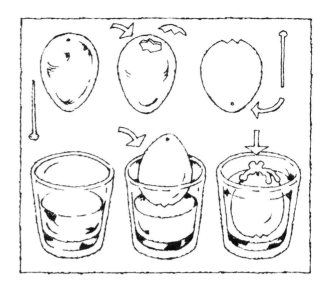

The chick pricks a hole in the wall of the air chamber to breathe.

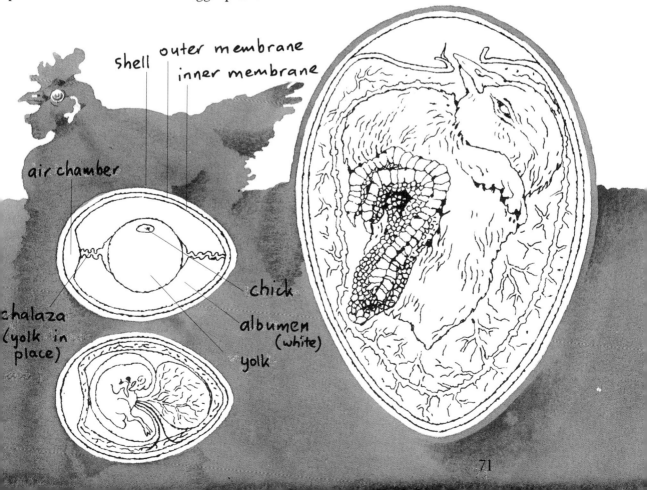

shell

outer membrane

inner membrane

air chamber

chalaza
(yolk in place)

chick

albumen (white)

yolk

71

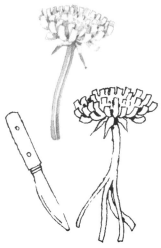

Carefully cut the lower half of a dandelion stem into quarters, and put it in water. The four cut pieces will curl up because of the flower's suction force. The inside of the stem absorbs water more strongly than the outside.

Split the stem of a white flower half way up. Put one half in red ink and the other in green. In a short time one side of the flower will turn green, and the other side red. Again the suction force has been at work.

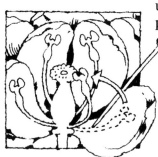

Gently prod barberry flower stamens from underneath with a pin. If they're ripe, they'll curl up at once. This is how insects get their helping of pollen. The same thing happens with African hemp.

Tricks

Plants and animals are full of forces which they need to germinate, to grow, to hunt and to survive. We can use these forces for tricks.

When you've squeezed a lemon, your whole hand will smell of it. This is because drops of oil squeezed out of it remain on your skin. Oil is inflammable. Squeeze a bit of lemon peel and hold a lighted match close to it; the sparks will fly off.

When a fly falls into water, it looks as if it's dead. This isn't necessarily the case. Rescue the insect and sprinkle it with salt. After a quarter of an hour it'll pick up again and fly off. Salt attracts water and absorbs it from the fly's blocked air passages.

Plants breathe through tiny holes or pores in their leaves. You can't see these without a microscope, but they can be demonstrated. Fix the stalk of a water lily leaf to the end of a bicycle pump. Tape the connection to stop it leaking. Put the leaf upside down on the bottom of a bowl of water and hold it down with a couple of pebbles. As you gently pump, you'll see where the pores are from the air bubbles rising to the surface.

You can eat peas or you can use them for practical jokes. Fill a jar with dried peas, pour water in up to the top and hide it near your victim's bed. The peas drink the water, swell and push each other out. Tick! The first pea falls over the edge. A couple of minutes later, another tick! And so on, just loud enough and frequently enough to spoil their sleep!

73

Creepy crawlies

Some odd-looking creatures live on the ground. Most don't like daylight and they crawl away from dryness. They only really feel happy when it's dark and damp. They live at night and hide under stones and rotting leaves in the daytime.

If you lift a stone in a damp place, a little insect called a woodlouse will crawl away in surprise. They may not look pleasant, but in fact they're clean, interesting creatures who share their preference for stones and rotting leaves with ground beetles, spiders and earthworms.

You can pick up most of these creatures in your hand but it's even easier with a vacuum jar. Fit a cork to a jar and bore two holes in it. Put a piece of tubing through each hole; one should be a little shorter than the other and have a small nylon bag (made from nylon stocking) fitted to it. Put the cork on the jar, position the longer tube above your quarry and suck on the shorter tube. When you do this, the creature is sucked up the other tube and into the jar. At nighttime, when you're asleep and the insects are awake, let traps do the work for you. The simplest is a wet pile of paper or a flowerpot turned upside down and filled with hay. The next day they'll be filled with worms and such like. A hollowed-out potato with a small entrance is also effective. Or make a trap in the ground by burying a jar up to its neck in the soil. Put a raised cover over it to keep out the rain. Most insects will fall into the jar anyway; others will need a piece of fruit or meat to entice them. Empty all the traps in the morning, count how many creatures of each sort you've caught and then set them free. Compare the numbers in your logbook with catches from other places and seasons.

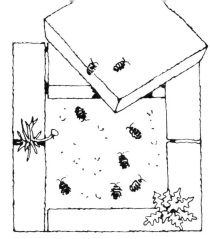

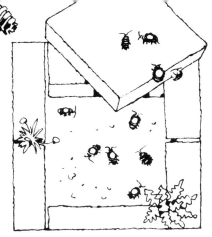

When you lift up a tile or stone, the woodlice will scurry off in all directions. They may look as if they're moving aimlessly, but in fact they are trying to find another dark, clammy spot as quickly as possible.

Mark woodlice with nail polish and search for them that night by lamplight. Better still, use luminous paint and make the beetles shine like glow-worms!

How many of the woodlice you marked are back at base the next morning? Where are the rest? Compare results after a dry night and a wet one.

You can sieve creatures from the soil. Spoon some rotting leaves into a strainer, shake it and put what's left in the sieve on to a sheet of white paper.
You can also extract the creatures automatically. Put a small pile of decaying matter on some wire-netting. Put the netting on top of a funnel and set the funnel in the mouth of a bottle. Then place the bottle under a strong light. The dryness and light will chase the insects from the leaves and into the bottle.

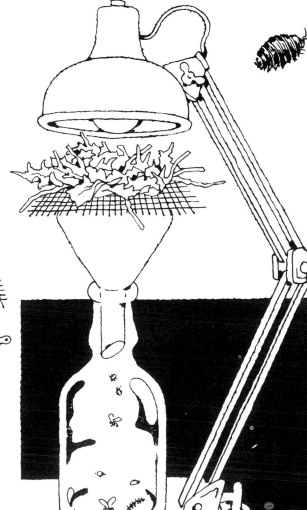

MAKE SOMETHING FROM IT

Nature is beautiful. It'd be difficult to find anyone who'd say that forests were ugly or a lark's song harsh. People like the countryside and they like being given flowers.

If you want to make something beautiful, why not use natural materials? Museums are filled with wood carvings and ivory ornaments and tapestries. American Indians, the Inuit (the proper word for Eskimos) and many other peoples used to be entirely dependent on plant and animal products.

Buffalo provided the Plains Indians with just about everything they needed. The skin was cured and made into leather, tom-toms and teepees; the hair was braided to make ropes and halters; the bones used as pestles or needles. The Indian people drank from the buffalo's horns, used its hooves as clubs for weapons, and, finally, roasted its flesh over a fire made from its own dried manure.

Quite aside from their beauty, natural materials have the advantage of never running out. Each year trees bear fruit and each year lambs are born and make new wool. Minerals from the ground, like iron and oil, are another story. The more people root around beneath the earth's surface, the sooner the earth's resources will be exhausted. The search is already on for a fuel substitute which can be grown. Sugar-beet, which releases good-quality fuel (alcohol) when it is burned, is one such alternative.

Food is the easiest natural product to make. Radishes, onions, peas and other vegetables are easy to grow in a garden, or if you have no garden, you could sow cress (see p.44) in a dish on the windowsill, as well as lettuces and tomatoes in plant pots.

Wood is a pure natural product. It is to a tree what a skeleton is to an animal, its frame. It's also through the wood of the roots that water streams up into the leaves of a living tree. How is it that a tree gets wider and wider when it only grows from the top of its trunk and the tips of its branches? (see p.67). This is because there is a thin layer between the wood and the bark which manufactures wood on the inside and bark on the outside. In winter, when the tree has no leaves, growth ceases. As a result, you can see exactly how old a tree is when it is cut down. Each pale ring in the stump corresponds to one spring's growth. Because wood is usually sawn lengthwise, these yearly rings show up in planks of wood as long stripes. Knots in the plank are where branches used to be.

Human beings have always envied animals their lovely warm skins, and they still kill some animals to make fur coats. Such killing is unnecessary. It is also endangering the very survival of animals like the snow leopard. Wool is just as warm, and sheep don't need to be killed for their wool, only sheared each year for the new growth. Rabbits and goats provide wool too, and people have even been known to spin dogs' hair – though they had problems once the sweaters were knitted. Apparently all the dogs in the area came up for a sniff! Cotton comes from a plant, from cotton balls, in fact, whose real job is to distribute the cotton plant's seed on the wind. There's no such thing as a linen plant; linen comes from a fibrous plant called flax. How can you tell if a garment is made of wool, cotton or linen? You could always look at the label, but it's more interesting finding out for yourself. If you can find a loose thread or strand, hold it in the flame of a match. You'll recognize wool at once because the smell of wool burning is just like the smell of one of your hairs burning (try it; pull out a hair and hold that in the flame too). This is because wool is made from the same horny tissue as our skin and nails. Linen and cotton burn more cleanly to a powder, almost without any smell. You can distinguish them from each other because linen is shiny and doesn't stretch, while cotton stretches and isn't shiny.

You may have a thread that melts instead of burning, and smells of chemicals. Then it's a synthetic cloth made in a factory, like nylon, acrylic, polyester, and so on. These are often mixed with wool or cotton to combine the advantage of synthetics (their strength) with those of natural fabrics, which are more comfortable to wear because they "breathe".

Wool is warm because it traps a layer of air which keeps in body warmth. Animals with a woolly coat are well off. What about birds with their feathers? Next time you find a feather, put it to a lighted match. It gives off the same smell as wool. So feathers are made of the same horny tissue. They trap the air too. Which is better, hairs or feathers? To find out, you'd need to put on a wool coat and then a feather one. You may have tried already, in bed! A blanket is a hair coat (from a mammal, the sheep), and an eiderdown is a feather coat (from a bird, the duck). The eiderdown wins; light and yet warm. Feathers are better. Now you know, you can use this to your advantage. Fill a cap with down and you'll never have cold ears again.

A tree-house

The best hideouts are tree houses, high up in the branches where you can see everything and everyone but they can't see you through the leaves. You can even hide the revealing rope-ladder by rolling it up behind you.

A tree house makes a wonderful hideout or clubhouse. You can also use it as a hide, to watch animals. You're at the same height as the birds, and animals on the ground don't see you because they look to the front and sides rather than up. Sunrise is the best time to go up and watch.

The house's floor needs to rest on three beams which you should lash firmly to the three trees. At least one of the beams should rest in a fork of two branches for extra support. The main drawing on the right shows how to fasten the floor to the beams. If you've got enough poles, you could use them to make walls. Otherwise, use sacking, straw matting or weave branches together.

While a roof isn't absolutely necessary, it does add a finishing touch. When you've got the hang of lashing wood together, you might make a bench and a small table where you can write in your log. Use branches to hang things from. To improve camouflage, weave branches together at intervals.

To begin with, you need three trees growing close together. It may be more difficult to get permission to build a hut in them. With any luck, the owner won't mind, as long as you promise only to use rope, and no nails. The drawing at the bottom of the opposite page shows how to lash two pieces of wood together. Fix one end of the rope with the rope-ladder knot (described below). Wind the rope across the two crossed poles. Repeat this a few times, then do it from the other direction (1). Now pull the rope through between the poles several times, pull it tight and tie it off with a rope-ladder knot (2).

You need 20 inch/50 cm lengths of wood for the rungs of the rope-ladder. Knot them across the two ropes using the rope-ladder knot (see diagrams 1-4 below).
Make a loop in the rope (1), make another loop next to it (2), put the second loop behind the first (3), push the rung through both loops (4) and pull the rope taut. The knot will tighten.

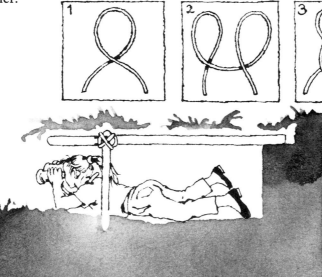

Find a ledge on a hillside for a lookout post. Make a roof for the shelter by lashing together poles and branches, and camouflage it with leaves and twigs. Once that's done, you can lie underneath on your tummy, hidden from view.

Ash is good for making bows with, as is chestnut. Cut a supple branch 1 yard (1m.) long and stretch string across it. Hazelnut wood is best for arrows. Make them 20 inches (50cm) long. Whittle one end to a point, and notch the other end for the bowstring to fit into. Cut a chicken's feather down the middle and then crossways and glue these four pieces to the arrow as shown below.

Fruit as decoration

The apples, cauliflowers and cucumbers laid out temptingly at the supermarket are a feast for the eye. They positively glow with health. At home they're washed and then put into bowls and racks, waiting to be eaten. After all, that's what they were bought for, isn't it? Usually, yes, but this time they're going to go on being a feast for our eyes and not our tongues.

Not all flowers have to be put in water in a vase. Some look even lovelier, their tints more subtle, when they have been dried. Why not use vegetables and fruit for decoration too? They can be just as beautiful and they're often cheaper too.

Use the inside leaves of red cabbage, the thinnest ones without any thick veins. Thread them with string and hang them up. They'll be dry in three days. Do the same with white and green cabbage and you'll have a cabbage bouquet. Why not try adding dried flowers to it?

Many fruits look even more beautiful inside than out. When you cut them, you can see the regular patterns made by the segments and seeds. These are easiest to see if the slices are thin. Try to cut them so thin that you can see through them. Stick them to the window so the sun can shine through. You won't need glue; if you throw them at the window from close by, they'll stick. Different fruits have different patterns, and you can also get several patterns from one fruit by cutting it in various ways – across, lengthwise, and diagonally. Be sure to clean up – and not leave a rotten mess for your poor parents!

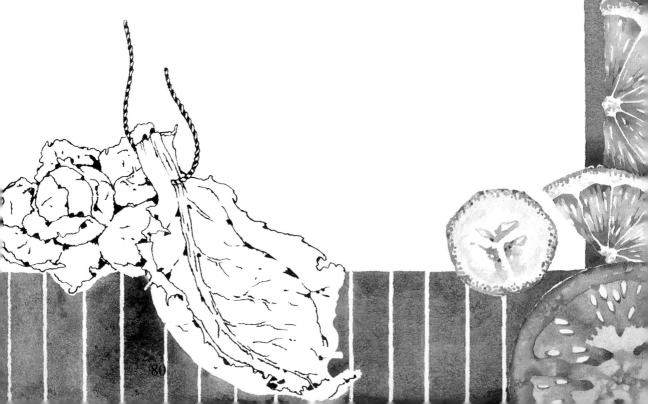

Braiding

Most of us have learned how to braid or plait and do basic weaving by the time we're eight or nine, but these things weren't only meant for children. The American Indians braided quivers for their arrows, and long ago in Egypt people went to sea in boats made of woven grass.

These skills have never died out. Many of us prefer baskets to boxes or bags – there are dogs' baskets, linen baskets, fruit and flower baskets. They're cheap because the materials are cheap and you don't need nails or glue to make them. Craft shops usually sell a range of raffia, rushes and cane. You'll need to wet the last two before you can work with them. But it's more fun to hunt for materials than to buy them. Willow twigs (soak in water for a week) and vine tendrils are best for strong baskets. You can make other things from grass,

straw, reeds or the leaves round corn. Dry the maize leaves in the sun and cut them into strips. Sprinkle them with water before you begin to work. You can also weave them green and let them dry later in the sun.

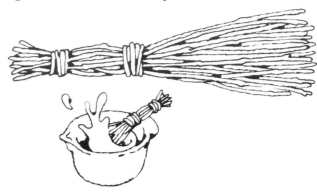

Thin birch twigs are strong and supple enough to weave. Or try making a special birch whisk for the kitchen. All you need to do is cut about forty twigs the same length, and tie them together with two lengths of thick string, as in the picture.

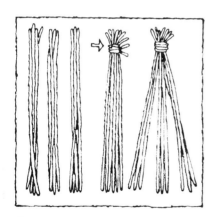

Straw is too thin to work with, so it first has to be braided into thicker strands. (Braiding and plaiting are different words for the same thing.) Take a bunch of straw and tie it together at one end. Divide the bunch into three.

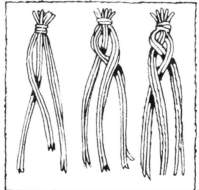

Now start braiding/plaiting. Bring the left bunch over the middle, then the right bunch over the middle (previously the left), and so on: left over middle, right over middle. Tie the ends together when you have finished.

Coil the braid and sew it together with needle and thread to make a small round table mat. You can make a corn dolly from one braid. Loosen it at the bottom and spread it to make the dolly's skirt. Tie a bunch of straw at either end and pull it through the braid to make the arms. Finally, wind some straw around the body.

The fruit basket below has been made from rushes, which you can pick from river banks or buy in a craft shop. Keep the rushes moist, but not too wet, while you work. First you need to make a loom. A piece of bendy cardboard will do, 1 yard x 1 foot (100 x 30cm). Cut notches along the shorter sides every ¾ inch. (Or every other cm.) Stretch rushes across the loom.

These should be cut into 2 foot 6 inch (85cm) lengths and be knotted at both ends. Put the knots behind the notches. These rushes are the "warp". Now start weaving 6 inches (15 cms) from one end of the loom with the rest of the rushes, the "weft". Weave the first rush under a warp rush, over the next, under and over, and so on till it's finished, then continue with the next

rush. To make the join, go back over the last few weaves of the previous rush. Continue till you are 6 inches (15 cms.), from the other end of the loom and your weaving measures about 20 inches (50 cms). Take it off the loom. Fold the sides together at the end and bind the loose ends with the remains of the rushes. Now all you need to do is fill the basket with fruit.

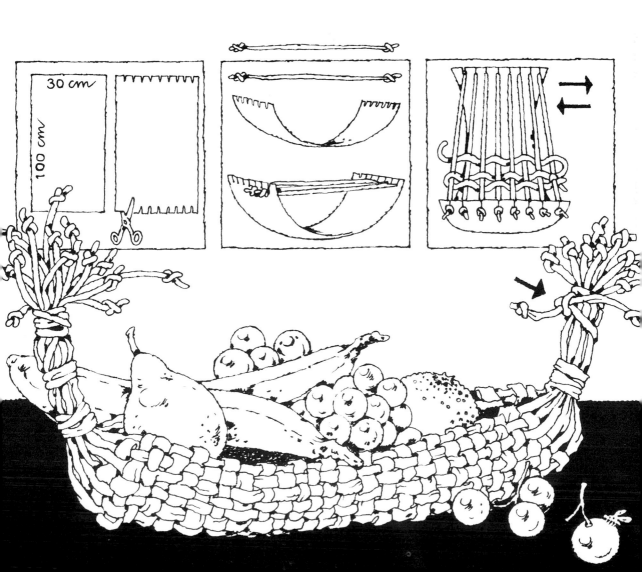

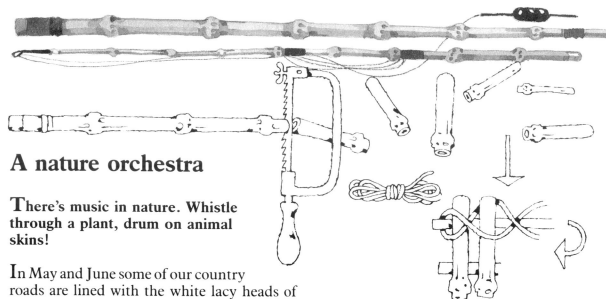

A nature orchestra

There's music in nature. Whistle through a plant, drum on animal skins!

In May and June some of our country roads are lined with the white lacy heads of cow parsley. Find a length of cow-parsley stem with a knob on it, cut it and blow down it. It makes a hollow sound, like bamboo. If you've got any old bamboo canes in the house, saw one into pieces, with a knob in each bit. Thinner pieces make high notes, wider ones low notes. Lash them together and make a set of pan-pipes.

Stretch a skin over a pot. Pig's bladder used to be used, but a sheet of plastic will do. Put a reed through the middle of the skin (see drawing below) and you've got an old Dutch instrument called a rumbling pot. If you wet your hands and rub them round the reed as you move it up and down, you'll soon find out why it's called that!

LEND A HAND

Plants and animals have always had hard lives. Think about a sparrow with a crust of bread. It looks up constantly from its food, always on the lookout for gulls, cats, and other sparrows. Hunger, thirst and disease are animals' constant companions. Only half the young birds which leave their nests in summer survive into the next year. In reality, the expression "as free as a bird" is meaningless. Many birds have to retreat to their own territory for safety. Even those which fly back and forth over different hemispheres aren't free because they fly along fixed air passages which makes them more like bus drivers following a pre-arranged route than carefree vagabonds. A plant, on the other hand, is tied to the same place all its life, wherever it happened to have landed as a seed. Plants' lives are usually short. If they're not smothered shortly after germination by nearby plants or by trees taking the light from them, they are eaten by animals or humans, or picked, or trampled on.

Even so, nature has survived for 3,000 billion years. From time to time, there were disasters – like the sudden extinction of dinosaurs – yet nature continued. The wolves have never eaten all the rabbits, and bacteria and fungi have always cleared away rubbish; no one variety of animal or plant has had the upper hand over another. However, things have been spoiled recently. Human beings are upsetting everything.

It all began with hunting. Humans went out shooting with their guns, and overdid it. They shot lions because they frightened them, beavers for their skins, kangaroos because they got in the way, wild boar for feasts, zebras so that their heads could adorn the mantelpiece. Hunting continues, (mainly now as "entertainment"!) for foxes, elephants, cougars, rabbits, and, most popular of all sports, for fish. Millions of fish die each year from the wounds they have received, and in many countries, swans die from swallowing the old discarded hooks that fishermen carelessly leave in rivers!

Plants and animals are affected as we use the world to suit ourselves. We build cities where once there were forests, we put up industrial parks where once there were green fields. Wetlands are drained and lose their wild flowers and waterfowl as more grain is sown. Tropical forest is being felled at the rate of one Scotland a year. (Look that up on a map and you'll see why so many people are worried.) And that's mainly to provide fields for cows to eat – for our hamburgers! Plants and animals cannot complain so it is up to us to do it for them. Some smart animals adapt. They forget their shyness and follow people. Where people live, there will always be something to eat and a place to sleep. Pigeons and even birds of prey swoop enthusiastically on the rubbish left lying around towns, and they nest just as happily on tall buildings as on their original high cliffs. Rats feel at home in the sewers, and housemites have as good a time in heated homes and tower blocks as they ever did in the tropics.

There are even some plants which benefit

from man. Canadian pondweed emigrated and is now the most common of all European water plants. Plantain, which grows along paths and in grass, a plant which can survive being trampled on, went in the other direction. North American Indians called the plant "white man's footstep" because it sprang out of the ground wherever the white colonists set foot.

Unfortunately most varieties are unable to save themselves. *Every day,* somewhere in the world, some species of plant or animal dies out, becomes extinct. Nature reserves have been set up all over the world to protect those that are left. Two and a half per cent of land in the world is protected. This is nowhere near enough. And besides, even in reserves, plants and animals are not safe as long as our air and water are polluted. This pollution comes from factory waste and from the chemicals sprayed on the fields, from exhaust fumes, chemicals and detergents in our water and from the chemicals and rubbish we throw down the sink and put in our bins. The most dangerous poisons of all and radioactive waste are dumped far out at sea, and many people shudder to think what would happen if the containers leaked.

You can help those concerned about nature and the environment by joining conservation organizations. Donations made to any of the national societies for instance, help them to protect areas of outstanding natural beauty in this country. The World Wildlife Fund collects money for reserves all over the world. Friends of the Earth works both locally and worldwide and will help inform you and build up your personal commitment. If you believe in spectacular action, Greenpeace is the one. Greenpeace members take rubber boats out on the high seas to obstruct whalers and those dumping poison. You won't be able to go with them but you can help by collecting money or signatures for their campaigns. If you prefer to go it alone, then why not help birds (see pages 88 and 90) or measure pollution (see p.92). And remember to care for every plant, insect or animal you come in contact with. Part of the real solution to the world's conservation is going to need personal commitment and less greed from millions of individuals all over the world.

Feed them

We'd probably all like to talk to the animals. Since we can't, we feed them, and that brings us into some sort of contact. Eating is a language all living creatures understand, which doesn't mean that we should feed them all! You shouldn't feed animals in zoos, for instance, because they're on special diets. It's better to feed animals which really need it, like birds in winter.

Feeding birds is useful for you because you'll be able to get a closer look when they come for the food. Sketch them in your logbook. All sorts will come at first, pushy ones like sparrows and, when it gets colder, shyer birds like thrushes. Each day note down which birds came and what the weather was like, what they ate and how. Although starlings like fat, they hate big lumps of it. Greedy birds are jostled aside by even greedier ones: sparrows by starlings, starlings by crows. Which comes out on top at your bird table? Sparrows always come in groups, robins come alone. How do other birds come? Finches love peanuts, but do any other birds like them?

Remember that you aren't the only one who likes birds. Cats do too. Be sure they can't get at the birds you're attracting, or you'll be feeding the cats instead of the birds.

Many birds eat insects, but there aren't a lot about in winter. Luckily, insectivorous birds also enjoy oil and fat. Peanuts and sunflower seeds contain a lot of oil. Leave dead sunflower heads out for the birds, and make peanut chains with unsalted, unroasted peanuts. To make a lump of fat for the birds, first melt down some fat, sprinkle in birdseed, pour it into an old yoghurt pot and put in a length of wire. When the fat has hardened, scoop it out of the pot with a knife and hang it up by the wire. Hang up a coconut too, having first bored a hole in it 1¼ inches (3 cm.) wide. You can also hang up apple cores and the bones from chops.

Birdhouses aren't much good. The roof blocks the view, both yours and the birds, who need to be able to watch out for danger. A table is better. Ours is just a 16 inch (40 cm.) square plank on a pole – so that cats can't jump up. The ridge round the edges prevents mess and the wire netting keeps the cat away. Food may get wet of course, but it won't go rotten if you clear away the remains every night. Put your table near a tree so that the birds can check from there that the coast is clear before flying down to feed.

However beautiful your table, there will always be birds which prefer feeding from the ground, so scatter food there too. Don't put down more than the birds can get through in a day.

Feed them unsalted peanuts, oats, bits of fruit, wholemeal breadcrumbs, raisins, cooked potatoes, and mixed bird seed. Lots of dry white bread and highly-spiced food are dangerous. You can collect seeds yourself. Gather the feathery seed heads of thistles when the flower has blown, catkins, and winged maple seeds. Keep all your apple, pear and melon seeds. Store berries after drying them first in a low oven. In this way all through the year, you can store food for winter. What about spring? In spring you can see which plants have started to grow from the seeds that the birds leave lying on the ground.

Give them a home

At the end of winter we can close our bird restaurant and put away the feeder because now the birds can find food themselves. There's plenty for them because not all the birds will have survived the winter. Spring is the season they make good their losses, laying eggs in nests for new birds to hatch. There's a snag though. There may be enough to eat but now there aren't enough places to build a nest, least of all hollow trees. Nowadays trees are often felled before they become hollow.

So we'll have to continue helping birds. We've given them a restaurant, now we'll build a bird hotel, a nesting box to take the place of a hollow tree.

Hang your nesting boxes up in February so that the birds know where to find them. The openings should face east. Check them every day. Have any birds arrived yet?

First the birds come to investigate. If they approve of the hotel, you'll soon see them flying in with pieces of straw in their beaks. Make a note of when this happens. Never disturb the birds by looking inside the nest. Listen instead. When do the young birds chirp for the first time? Now the parents are carrying food instead of straw. For half an hour each day count how often they fly in with food; they do this more and more frequently. Why? Follow the parents to see how far they fly for food. How many miles does that mean they cover in one day? One day activity round the nesting box ceases, because the young birds have all flown away. You'll miss them. They'd begun to feel like family.

Wooden nesting boxes come in all shapes and sizes, a different kind for each bird. The box below is suitable for several kinds of birds – you'll soon find out which. Use wood ¾ inch (2 cm.) thick. Don't paint it. Drill four holes in the base for water to drain away. The measurements given are in cms.

Put a wooden box, made from three pieces of wood, under the gutter of the roof for sparrows. It's better than having them nesting under the roof.

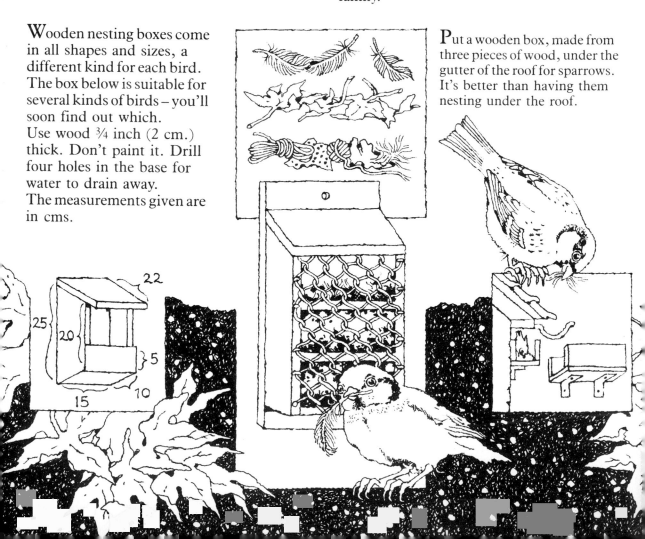

Hollow trees don't come in pre-arranged sizes and many birds which breed in hollows are not very particular. They'll make their nests in an old bucket or can, if they have to. You could help by hanging one or two in the branches among the leaves. Punch four holes in the base with a hammer and nail for water to drain away, unless there's a spout, in which case hang the container spout-side down.

For barn-owls, tie a cylinder about 2½ inches (7 cms.) wide – the sort they send posters in – to the branch of a tree. Cut off the end at an angle to make a roof and cover the top with plastic as protection from the rain.

House martins like nesting in old sheds, near the door. Help them by putting up a wooden nesting table, 6 inches (15 cms.) square. Put it near the roof and by the door of an outside shed. The birds will make their nests themselves, but again you could help by supplying a shop, such as the one you see on the opposite page: a box with three shelves and a wire-netting front. Fill the shelves with hay, moss, pieces of string, dried leaves, feathers, strands of wool and dog's hair. Hang it where your hotel guests can see it. What service!

15

15

A finger on the pulse

All is not well in the environment. Air and water are polluted and this causes problems for plants and animals. You cannot nurse the environment back to health on your own – there are people specially appointed for that, but you can help by keeping an eye on it.

How are things where you live? From now on, keep your eyes and nose open. Unfortunately, not all pollution can be smelled, that's what's so frustrating. Even so, you don't need a laboratory to demonstrate that it's there. The best pointers, the plants and animals around you, are free.

Lichens and mosses, which grow mainly on old walls and trees, are the best indicators of how clean the air is. Lichens are plants which have no roots, stems or flowers. Because they have no roots, they absorb the rain directly, dirt and all, and this makes them vulnerable to air pollution. In general if an area has a great "species diversity" i.e. many different types of lichen, it is not polluted. But some species are more vulnerable than others.

– Where there is still beard moss on trees (1), all is well. The air could hardly be *cleaner.* (Although it is not very sensitive to acid rain.)
– At the first signs of pollution, beard moss disappears and a bushy kind of lichen takes its place. (2)
– If the lichens only grow on stones (3) and not on the trees, the air is usually polluted.
– If there are no lichens to be seen anywhere and tree trunks just look green from the algae growing on them (4), things are in a bad way.

Water pollution can be measured with a fishing net (landing net) and a shallow white bowl to examine your catch in.

– If you see creatures with three threadlike tails (5), the water is clean as clean. These are mayfly. Caddis fly larvae are also very sensitive to polluted water.

– Shrimps (6) usually live only in clean water.

– A large number of water lice (7) indicates polluted water.

– Tubifex (8) and bloodworms, which are used as food in aquariums, can survive in all kinds of water, including very polluted water. They take the last bits of oxygen.

– Almost nothing can live once the oxygen has gone, and the water starts to stink.

Put twelve bottle-caps on a white sheet of cardboard and take one away every day. When the air is polluted, the first patches will be darker than the others.

Compare air pollution on the side of your city wherever the wind usually comes from – with that on the other side of town, where it usually goes. Compare pollution in a river on either side of a factory which discharges waste into it. Dead fish are an indication that chemicals are being illegally discharged. Ask fishermen whether they've been catching more or fewer fish lately. Plant growth in a river is not necessarily a good sign. It may be there because too much artificial fertiliser has been washed into the river from the land. On hot days, so much algae grows in water like this that the river can look as green as pea soup.

6

7

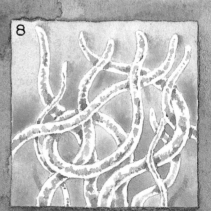

8

INDEX